Essential Histories

The Anglo-Afghan Wars
1839–1919

Gregory Fremont-Barnes

First published in Great Britain in 2009 by Osprey Publishing,
PO Box 883, Oxford, OX1 9PL, UK
PO Box 3985, New York, NY 10185-3985, USA
Email: info@ospreypublishing.com

Osprey Publishing is part of the Osprey Group.

© 2009 Osprey Publishing Ltd.

Transferred to digital print on demand 2014.

First published 2009
3rd impression 2013

Printed and bound by
Cadmus Communications, USA.

A CIP catalogue record for this book is available from the
British Library.

ISBN: 978 1 84603 446 6

Page layout by Myriam Bell Design, France
Index by Fineline Editorial Services
Typeset in GillSans and 1TC Stone Serif
Maps by The Map Studio
Originated by PDQ Media, Bungay, UK

The Woodland Trust
Osprey Publishing are supporting the Woodland Trust, the UK's
leading woodland conservation charity, by funding the
dedication of trees.

www.ospreypublishing.com

Author's note
Readers should note that consistent transliteration from
Pashtun, Dari and other Afghan languages into English is
problematic, particularly with respect to place names and
family names, many of which bore different renderings in the
19th century than they do today, thus: Kandahar/Qandahar;
Kabul/Cabool/Cabul/Cabaul/Qabul; Jellalabad/Jalalabad;
Jugdulluk/Jagdalak; Khoord Cabul Pass/Khurd-Kabul Pass; Ali
Musjid/Ali Masjid; Gilzai/Gilzye, etc. The author has therefore
adopted the most commonly accepted form or that which most
closely reflects local pronunciation.

Historical note
Readers should be aware that until 1858 Indian affairs were
managed jointly between Crown officials and those of the East
India Company (EIC). In London, the apparatus of the former
consisted of the Secretary of State for War and the Colonies,
who issued instructions to the Governor-General in Calcutta
and the Board of Control, whose president, as a cabinet
minister, was accountable to Parliament. In Calcutta was the
EIC, originally a chartered company with purely commercial
concerns, but which by the 18th century exercised wide
political and military control over much of the subcontinent on
behalf of the Crown. The EIC maintained its own armies, which
served in conjunction with those of the Crown, all commanded
by a cabinet-appointed commander-in-chief answerable to the
War Office in London.

In 1858, the EIC was disbanded, the Crown assuming all
authority over India via the Secretary of State for India, who sat
in the cabinet, a civilian viceroy, and a commander-in-chief of
the newly established, British-led Indian Army.

Glossary

Abattis	Defence work consisting of a tree with sharpened branches, felled so that its branches point outwards
Doolie	Covered stretcher, litter or palanquin for the evacuation of the wounded
Feringee	A disparaging term for a European
Ghazi	Fighter for the Faith who has killed an infidel
Havildar	Indian infantry sergeant
Infidel	Unbeliever
Jezail	Long-barrelled matchlock musket carried by tribesmen
Jihad	Holy war
Jirga	Assembly of tribal elders or representatives
Kotal	Mountain pass
Lakh	100,000 rupees, the equivalent of £10,000 today
Mullah	Religious teacher, leader or holy man
Nullah	Small valley or ravine
Poshteen	Sheepskin jacket with a fleece lining
Sangar	Stone breastwork
Sepoy	Indian infantryman
Sirdar	Commander
Sowar	Indian cavalry trooper
Wazir	Chief minister or advisor

Essential Histories

The Anglo-Afghan Wars
1839–1919

Contents

Introduction

On 13 January 1842, a British officer, perched on the rooftop of the fortress at Jalalabad in eastern Afghanistan, spotted a lone horseman, hunched over and exhausted, ponderously approaching. The rider was Dr William Brydon, an army surgeon and the sole survivor of an Anglo-Indian army of 16,000 soldiers and camp followers that had left Kabul only a week before – now utterly annihilated by exhaustion, frostbite and almost continuous attack by Afghan tribesmen. The total destruction of the Army of the Indus exemplified the nature of fighting in this forbidding and hostile environment, populated by fiercely independent, ferocious war-minded peoples, indeed perhaps the most formidable guerrilla fighters in the world. To the British, Indian and Gurkha soldier of this period, Afghanistan would become a byword for savage and cunning enemies, inhospitable climate, bitter winters, scorching summers and rugged and beautiful terrain, including deep ravines and precipitous mountains, all ideal for mounting defence and ambush. Afghanistan appeared a seemingly unconquerable place where heroism, cowardice and sacrifice abounded, and where death awaited those foolish enough to venture across the frontier without the most careful attention paid to strategy and proper supply, organization and transport. The country's infamous reputation for causing suffering on campaign inspired Rudyard Kipling to produce one of the most popular poems of the age:

The British camp at Pezwan, September 1880. (Author's collection)

When you're wounded and left on
   Afghanistan's plains,
An' the women come out to cut up
   what remains,
Jest roll to your rifle an' blow out
   your brains,
An' go to your Gawd like a soldier.

Yet if Afghanistan was to prove the graveyard
of many a soldier, it was only one amongst
many of the conflicts waged by Britain
during Victoria's reign (1837–1901). Every
year of her reign saw her forces deployed
on campaign somewhere across the globe,
particularly in Africa and Asia, in an
uninterrupted series of colonial wars and
minor operations to protect British nationals
and British interests, shift a frontier in the
Empire's favour, suppress a mutiny or revolt,
or repel an attack. As the world's leading
imperial power, Britain waged these
campaigns without hesitation, and
with the full confidence of ultimate
victory against foes who were inevitably
numerically superior, yet technologically and
organizationally inferior. Such was the price
of maintaining and expanding the Empire,
of upholding the nation's pride in its own
perceived cultural, economic and political
superiority in the world – and usually at
relatively little cost.

Amongst all these conflicts, however, the
three Anglo-Afghan Wars (1839–42, 1878–81
and 1919) stand out. In military terms they
shared much in common with other British
campaigns – initial, sometimes even
catastrophic failure, but ultimate victory
in the field. Yet in political terms the wars
ended uneasily at best and disastrously at
worst, with an extension of British influence
but never extensive annexation or evidence
that the original aims could not have been
achieved through diplomacy alone. The wars
were marked by varying degrees of political
and military incompetence and brilliance,
disaster and triumph in rapid succession.
There were also plentiful examples of
supreme folly by politicians, who failed
to identify at the outset clear political
objectives or recognize that the solution

to the problem at the heart of the first two
conflicts, at least, could never lie in military
intervention alone.

Britain's fear of Russian expansion into
Afghanistan formed the backdrop of its first
two conflicts; in the first instance, fought
between 1839 and 1842, the Governor-
General of India insisted upon an invasion
even after the ostensible reason for hostility
had passed. The consequences were
devastating, for after their initially successful
campaign, in which Anglo-Indian forces
imposed on the Afghans an unacceptable
ruler, they proceeded down the road of
folly by attempting to control the country
through mere occupation. The result is well
known: unable to hold even Kabul, the army
withdrew towards India, only to meet its
inevitable demise along the snow-bound
roads and passes en route to Jalalabad.
Subsequent operations went some way
towards resurrecting British prestige, but
the lesson was clear: despite a century of
military success in India, British arms were
not invincible, and Afghanistan could not
long be held under foreign sway.

Nevertheless, Anglo-Russian rivalry in
Central Asia led to a second British invasion
of Afghanistan (1878–81), leading to yet
another partial and temporary – though
militarily more successful – occupation,
for effective control, especially of the vast
countryside, again proved impossible.
As in the first war, the British would
suffer a crushing defeat, at Maiwand,
with their reputation only restored after
achieving a decisive victory over the
Afghans at Kandahar. But the war would
finish on the basis of compromise, with
Britain controlling the foreign policy of
Afghanistan, a point that largely contributed
to a third, but much shorter and less costly
conflict in 1919, when Afghanistan sought
to throw off the last vestiges of British
control over its internal affairs.

The origins of Britain's wars in
Afghanistan may be traced to its obsession
with the vulnerability of the Indian
subcontinent – its greatest imperial
possession – to possible invasion by

Afghan tribesmen lie in ambush among rocks during the Second Afghan War. Eastern Afghanistan is ideal ground for irregular warfare. (National Army Museum)

Russia via Afghanistan. Known as 'the Great Game', the competition for influence in Central Asia fuelled the fears of two generations of Victorian soldiers, politicians, colonial administrators and the public. When shortly after the First Afghan War the border of British India expanded to include what became known as the North-West Frontier – a land peopled largely by Afghans of various tribes – the military commitment of Britain and the Raj perforce expanded, removing any further buffer with Afghanistan and drawing into the Empire a region notorious for its volatile, warlike population of disparate tribes. These tribes, while largely hostile to one another, generally made common cause to oppose the invading *feringees* (a disparaging term for a European). Over the course of a century of British rule, which concluded with the independence of India and its partition in 1947, maintaining security along the North-West Frontier (now the 'tribal areas' of western Pakistan) would require the dispatch of dozens of punitive operations. In effect, the Anglo-Afghan Wars may more accurately be described as three conflicts conducted in Afghanistan proper, and a series of sporadic, low-intensity operations conducted between Anglo-Indian forces and Afghan tribesmen along the North-West Frontier.

Though little is remembered of these conflicts – indeed, the third lasted but a few weeks and concluded nearly a century ago – their relevance to Britain's interests in the region stands out all the more prominently since the deployment of its armed forces in the country in November 2001.

Chronology

First Afghan War, 1839–42

1836 **4 March** Lord Auckland appointed Governor-General of India

1837 **20 June** Princess Victoria succeeds to the British throne at the age of 18
September Captain Alexander Burnes arrives in Kabul on mission to Dost Mohamed
1 December Persian siege of Herat begins
19 December Ivan Vitkevich, Tsar's special envoy, arrives in Kabul

1838 **1 October** Auckland issues a manifesto declaring intention to restore Shah Shuja to the Afghan throne by force
10 December Bengal division marches from Ferozepore in India

1839 **19 February** Anglo-Indian forces reach west bank of the Indus
10 March Sir John Keane's Army of the Indus enters the Bolan Pass, beginning the invasion of Afghanistan
3 May Army of the Indus concentrated at Kandahar; Shah Shuja crowned Amir
23 July Keane's forces storm fortress of Ghazni
6 August Army of the Indus enters Kabul and installs Shah Shuja as new Amir; Dost Mohamed, the deposed Amir, flees north to the Hindu Kush
December Dost Mohamed surrenders to the British

1840 **Spring** British build cantonment outside Kabul

1841 **2 November** Start of anti-Shuja revolt in Kabul; Burnes, the British resident, his brother and others murdered in Kabul
22 November Akbar Khan, Dost Muhamed's eldest son, arrives in Kabul to lead the ongoing rebellion
23 November Brigadier-General John Shelton is soundly defeated by Afghan rebels in the Behmaru Hills
11 December Anglo-Afghan agreement; British to withdraw from Kabul on the 15th under safe conduct
23 December Sir William Macnaghten and an aide are murdered by Akbar Khan during negotiations respecting the safe withdrawal of the Kabul garrison

1842 **1 January** Major-General William Elphinstone, British commander-in-chief in Afghanistan, concludes an agreement with Akbar Khan for the safe conduct of all British troops to Peshawar
6 January Anglo-Indian garrison of 4,500 troops and 12,000 civilians leaves Kabul on march to Jalalabad
13 January Last stand of the 44th Foot at Gandamak
10 January Akbar Khan takes Elphinstone and Shelton prisoner
April Shah Shuja is murdered in Kabul
7 April Sir Robert Sale, at Jalalabad, makes a major sortie against his besiegers in hope of assisting the advance of a relief column under Major-General George Pollock
16 April Pollock's force relieves the garrison at Jalalabad
23 April Elphinstone dies in captivity at Tezeen
20 August Pollock leaves Jalalabad in an advance on Kabul
15 September Pollock's troops retake Kabul
12 October The 'Avenging Army' leaves Kabul for Peshawar; Dost Mohamed later released from British custody and reinstated as Amir

oops reach

returns to his
roval

War, 1878–81

1878   2 November Lord Lytton, Viceroy of
India, sends Sher Ali, the Afghan Amir,
an ultimatum, demanding he accept a
British diplomatic mission in Kabul
22 November Major-General Sir
Samuel Browne captures the fortress
at Ali Masjid
24 November Browne occupies Dacca
2 December Major-General Frederick
Roberts takes Peiwar Kotal
13 December Sher Ali appoints as
regent his son, Yakub Khan, and flees
his capital
20 December Browne occupies
Jalalabad

1879   8 January Major-General Sir Donald
Stewart occupies Kandahar

21 January Stewart occupies
Kalat-i-Gilzai
21 February Sher Ali dies; his son,
Yakub Khan, agrees to negotiate
6 April Gandamak occupied by
Anglo-Indian forces
8 May Yakub Khan arrives at the
British camp at Gandamak
26 May Treaty of Gandamak, bringing
an apparent end to the conflict
24 July Sir Pierre Louis Napoleon
Cavagnari enters Kabul
3 September Attack on the British
Residency at Kabul
26 September Yakub Khan leaves
Kabul
6 October Battle of Charasia
13 October Roberts enters Kabul
28 October Yakub Khan abdicates
23 December Assault on Sherpur

British cavalry and horse artillery in action outside Kabul,
11 December 1879, when Brigadier-General Dunham
Massy, with only 200 officers and troopers of the
9th Lancers, about 40 Bengal Lancers and four guns of
the RHA, blundered into an Afghan force of thousands.

In the years between the three Anglo-Afghan wars, sporadic warfare continued in the rugged frontier territory. Here, as the Gordon Highlanders storm the Dargai Heights on 20 October 1897 – part of the Tirah campaign against an Afghan tribe, the Afridis – Piper Findlater continues to play despite his wounds, for which extraordinary act he received the Victoria Cross. (Author's collection)

1880   1 April Stewart leaves Kandahar for Kabul
19 April Battle of Ahmed Khel
2 May Stewart arrives in Kabul
22 July Abdur Rahman declared Amir
27 July Battle of Maiwand
6 August Ayub Khan besieges Kandahar
8 August Roberts leaves Kabul for Kandahar
11 August Stewart leaves Kabul for India
31 August Roberts marches into Kandahar
1 September Battle of Kandahar
1881   22 April British evacuate Kandahar

Third Afghan War, 1919

1919   3 May Afghan troops cross into India and occupy village of Bagh
9 May British forces attack the Afghans at Bagh
17 May Afghans abandon their defences at Dacca
27 May British troops capture Afghan fortress of Spin Baldak; Nadir Khan besieges Thal
31 May British agree to grant armistice requested by Afghans
3 June Armistice signed
8 August Treaty of Rawalpindi

Opposite page:
Shah Shuja (Shuja-ul-Mulk), whose installation as Amir of Afghanistan on 3 May 1839 formed the ostensible basis on which Anglo-Indian forces had invaded the country two months earlier. (National Army Museum)

Part I

The First Anglo-Afghan War
1839–42

Origins and background of the war

The origins of Britain's rivalry with Russia in Central Asia may be traced to the 1820s, when Russia began to expand south through the Caucasus into north-west Persia, a process unsuccessfully opposed by British diplomatic support for Persia and Turkey. By the early 1830s, Persia had become a virtual Russian satellite. To compensate for losses in the north-west, the Shah, with Russian encouragement, seized territory in western Afghanistan, specifically the region around Herat, ruled by Kamran, whose great-grandfather had taken it from Persia. In 1835, the Governor-General of India recognized in a memorandum for his superiors in London that Russia could expand into Afghanistan via its influence over Persia, thus imperilling British India:

> It is the interest of Russia to extend and strengthen the Persian Empire, which occupies a central position between the double lines of operation of the Autocrat to eastward and westward, and as Persia can never be a rival of Russia the augmentation of her strength can only increase the offensive means of Russia... What the Russian policy might be after taking possession of Herat it is unnecessary now to consider but it is impossible to den... ...ive at that point ... ally, the Ki... difficult t... she may... British I... joined... tribes... force o...

The Persians f... and Lord Palme... Secretary, had issue...

were not to attack Afghanistan at Russia's behest. Herat under Persian control could lead to the establishment of a base for further incursion into Afghanistan – at least as far as Kandahar – whence the Russians could reach India, either via Kabul and the Khyber Pass or south-east through the Bolan Pass. Thus under no circumstances was Britain prepared to tolerate Russia or a Russian-backed Persia establishing a presence in Afghanistan. This antagonism constituted what became known as the 'Great Game', with the First Afghan War as its opening manifestation.

As far as the newly appointed Governor-General of India, Lord Auckland, together with the East India Company (EIC) were concerned, the best means of obviating Russian influence in Afghanistan was to ensure that Dost Mohamed, the present Amir in Kabul, supported British interests in the region. The question posed before Auckland and his advisers in 1837 was whether or not Dost Mohamed satisfied this need.

The Shah of Persia, despite British warning, continued to maintain a close relationship with Russia, and launched a renewed campaign against Herat in late July 1837, laying siege to the city on 1 December, with resistance expected to be brief. British fears were heightened when, on the 19th, a Cossack officer by the name of Ivan Viktorovich Vitkevich, bearing a letter from Tsar Nicholas I who hoped to establish diplomatic relations with the Amir, arrived in Kabul. Dost Mohamed was less interested in a connection with Russia than in using the letter to his advantage in another way. Since September the British already had a special envoy at the Afghan capital in the form of Captain Alexander Burnes, sent by Auckland. Burnes had made his reputation as a result of his recently published account of his travels through Central Asia and Afghanistan, during the course of which journey he had established good relations with Dost Mohamed in 1830. Burnes was in Kabul on account of an appeal from the Amir for British aid in his quarrel with the powerful Sikh kingdom in the neighbouring Punjab, under their formidable ruler Ranjit Singh. Four years earlier the Sikhs had seized Peshawar, formerly the richest province in Afghanistan. The British were not entirely amenable to interfering between the Afghans and the Sikhs, for the latter were allies of the EIC by treaty. There was also no obvious advantage in meddling in a dispute between independent states, notwithstanding the fact that British India and the Punjab shared a common border. Such sentiments formed the basis of Auckland's message to Dost Mohamed, but he did express a strong desire to discuss trade between India and Afghanistan and the use of the Indus as a waterway to facilitate commerce. Burnes had therefore arrived in Kabul to encourage commercial relations.

Yet it was soon apparent that the Amir was not interested in discussing trade; his troops, under Akbar Khan, had recently returned following their failure to take the fort at Jamrud from the Persians. What he desired, instead, was British assistance in recovering Peshawar from the Sikhs, under Ranjit Singh. Burnes had no power to negotiate political terms and thus had to await further instructions. These were in fa on their way. Auckland had received from the Secret Committee of the EIC's Court of Directors a memorandum requiring him to monitor events in Afghanistan closely, with the specific intention of preventing the progress of Russian influence there. The means to accomplish this objective were left to him, but if he saw fit he was authorized to interfere in Afghan affairs directly.

Auckland was almost certainly the wrong person in whom to invest such wide powers, owing to his inexperience of Afghan affairs, while Burnes himself was only a junior officer with little knowledge of diplomatic affairs. Burnes received new instructions, drafted by

Sir William Macnaghten, Auckland's Chief Secretary, offering no clear negotiating powers and lacking detail beyond emphasizing the need to favour the interests of Ranjit Singh over those of Dost Mohamed, whom Burnes was to admonish not to begin negotiations with any other power over the issue of Peshawar. These instructions placed Burnes in a difficult position at Kabul; yet he understood the urgency of affairs, for Dost Mohamed had given him a copy of the Russian envoy's letter.

Burnes, in possession of his new instructions but aware that he must give priority to Sikh interests, informed Auckland that the Amir was on friendly terms with Britain, but he was chiefly interested in the recovery of Peshawar. Barring a change in British policy in the form of some accommodation with Dost Mohamed, they risked alienating the Amir, driving him into the arms of Russia in the pursuit of an alternative ally against the Sikhs. Burnes characterized Dost Mohamed as more inclined to Britain than to Russia, strengthening the case by enclosing the Tsar's letter in his dispatch back to Calcutta.

tan, whose reign
pted by exile
collection)

Mohamed Akbar Khan, eldest son of Dost Mohamed, who led the uprising in Kabul in late 1841 and promised to guarantee the safe passage of Elphinstone's army and camp followers back to Jalalabad. His helmet, mail and shield on his back are testament to the fact that Afghan forces proved formidable opponents despite their medieval equipment and lack of formal training. (National Army Museum)

a *volte face* in his policy, Britain would not offer him friendship. This hardening of the British attitude, and Dost Mohamed's need for an ally in his struggle against the Sikhs and to keep the Persians in check, led the Amir to turn to the Russians when, in April 1838, he met with Vitkevich. Burnes had been proved right and, with his mission over after seven months, the Scotsman returned to India.

In turn, Auckland viewed the developments as justifying his distrust of Dost Mohamed, and consequently led the Governor-General to consider the Amir's replacement with a new ruler favourably inclined both to the British and the Sikhs for the purpose of curbing either direct Russian or Russian-backed Persian influence in Afghanistan, so restoring the balance of British influence in Central Asia. The most suitable candidate appeared to be a previous Amir, the Shah Shuja-il-Mulk, who maintained friendly terms with Ranjit Singh and who, after his last attempt to retake his throne from Dost Mohamed in 1834, had settled in Ludhiana in western India under British protection. Both the EIC and the Sikh court argued strongly in favour of his suitability, and this insistence, together with unsubstantiated reports that he would be well received in the Afghan capital, was sufficient to persuade Auckland and Macnaghten that Shah Shuja ought to be placed on the throne. The British also entertained the hope that, with financial backing from the treasury in Calcutta, the Sikhs would provide the troops to install Shah Shuja in Kabul, for they had much to gain from his restoration: principally, recognition of Ranjit Singh's claim to territory on the western side of the Indus River, which Dost Mohamed claimed. Still, the notion that the Afghan people might not take kindly to their traditional enemies imposing on them a new foreign monarch does not appear to have figured in Auckland's calculations.

For the next three months, Burnes continued to advocate support for the A[...] that in India Auckland [...] were growing increas[...] the Afghan govern[...] Mohamed compl[...] plan over Pesha[...] Auckland's suspi[...] in fact hostile to[...] appeared to supp[...] Dost Mohamed ha[...] a diplomatic represe[...] which maintained a[...] the Persian army besieging[...] assistance in negotiating terms w[...] Furthermore, he was not prepared to reach an arrangement with Ranjit Singh. Without

Ranjit Singh was not, however, prepared to back this plan with his own forces, so while he initially supported the

Sir Alexander Burnes, assigned as British diplomatic representative at Kabul by Lord Auckland, the Governor-General of India. Burnes was killed by an Afghan mob on 2 November 1841. (Author's collection)

enterprise he negotiated different terms with Macnaghten, who agreed to furnish Company troops for the undertaking. The Sikhs were committed to nothing more than maintaining a reserve force at Peshawar for eventualities, the circumstances of which never became clear. In the end, Ranjit Singh did commit himself to the enterprise as a signatory to the tripartite Treaty of Simla, concluded in June 1838 between himself, Shah Shuja and the British, with the Sikhs receiving in turn a guarantee of possession of the trans-Indus territory. Shah Shuja was to be restored to his throne with British aid, after which he would agree to British control of his foreign policy – thus enabling London and Calcutta to ensure no undue Russian influence in Afghan affairs.

In a manifesto issued on 1 October, Auckland declared his intentions respecting Afghanistan, stated the reasons which justified British intervention – not least the corrupt malpractices and illegitimacy of Dost Mohamed's government – and stressed above all the security of British India. 'The welfare of our possessions in the East,' he announced, 'requires that we should have on our western frontier an ally who is interested in resisting aggression, and establishing tranquility, in the place of chiefs ranging themselves in subservience to a hostile power and seeking to promote schemes of conquest and aggrandizement.' The war, he went on, was not to be conducted with a view toward occupation or territorial aggrandizement; as proof of this pledge, British troops would withdraw from the country once Shah Shuja had been safely and rightfully installed.

Warring sides

The forces that Britain could bring to bear against the Afghan tribes were composed almost exclusively of those of the EIC. For the previous century these forces had enjoyed almost unhindered success in the field against indigenous Indian armies, some of whose troops took up employment in one of the Company's three separate standing armies, representing each presidency: Madras, Bombay and Bengal. The rank and file of these forces was drawn from the area in which they were recruited, and they trained, dressed and fought in the style of the British Army, with white officers in command.

By the time of the First Afghan War, each *sepoy* (infantry) company served under the command of a British captain or lieutenant, together with a British subaltern and two Indian officers who had risen from the ranks, with ten such companies composing a 'Native' battalion (or regiment, all such units comprising but a single battalion, unlike their counterparts in the British Army, which had two), under a major or lieutenant-colonel. A similar system existed for regiments of cavalry, where troopers were known as *sowars*. Amongst the 'local' and irregular corps, of which there were many in India, only the commanding officer, second-in-command and adjutant were British, Indians filling all the remaining officers' positions, with exclusively Indian troops beneath them. Regular campaigning, whether against fellow Indian forces or in the First Burmese War of 1824–25, had helped develop a strong bond of mutual respect and trust between the *sepoys* and their British officers, and Native units generally fought well and loyally – at least until much of the Bombay Army mutinied in 1857. There were also 'European' units maintained by the EIC, composed entirely of British (more specifically, mostly Irish) soldiers, such as the Bengal Horse Artillery.

When the First Afghan War began in 1839, the Bengal Army contained 69 regiments of *sepoys* and one of Europeans, each consisting of one battalion, as well as 15 local battalions, including three of Gurkhas: superb, highly reliable troops recruited from Nepal. The Madras presidency mustered 51 *sepoy* battalions, the Bombay presidency, 26. Cavalry serving in the Company's forces consisted of two types: regular regiments of light cavalry – three from Bombay, and eight each from the Bengal and Madras armies – outfitted, armed and trained like their counterparts in British light dragoon regiments, and irregular mounted units, of which Bengal supplied four and Bombay one. The Company had its own complement of artillery, both of foot and of horse (the distinction being that the crews of the former marched on foot, whereas those of the latter moved on horseback), composed entirely of European personnel. The Company also maintained an engineering capacity in the form of sappers and miners of both European and indigenous composition.

In addition to Company forces in British India, the Crown itself sent out from home depots its own troops – that is, regular forces

Baluchis in the Bolan Pass, 1842. (National Army Museum)

holding the Queen's commission – to serve in one of the presidency armies, numbering 20 battalions of infantry and four regiments of light cavalry. Troops posted to India generally spent most of their adult lives there, since the many months' travel to reach the subcontinent militated against regular rotation to another station. Thus, a regiment might remain in India for two decades or more, with wastage – from disease, especially cholera, but also heat, excessive drink, casualties or discharge – replaced by drafts of recruits sent out from Britain. Troops from home, once acclimatized and experienced on campaign, proved hardy and dependable, and together with their *sepoy* counterparts proved a formidable fighting force; their forebears had, after all, in conjunction with Company forces, conquered Bengal under Clive, southern India from the French and the sultans of Mysore, and later conquered the Mahrattas in the west.

Whether belonging to a Queen's regiment or a Company's, all units were organized and armed identically, their principal weapons consisting of the smoothbore, muzzle-loading flintlock musket and bayonet for the infantry, and the sabre or lance carried by the cavalry. Artillery was also smoothbore, field batteries consisting of six 6-pdrs, with heavier pieces, including mortars, reserved for siege operations, though mountainous terrain often rendered transportation of heavy artillery all but impossible. The infantry were dressed smartly yet impractically for the climate in heavy scarlet tunics, white cross belts, black leather pouches, haversacks and tall black shakos. They marched in closely ordered ranks, deployed shoulder-to-shoulder as at Waterloo a generation before and indeed as under Marlborough more than a century earlier, advancing in column but deploying for action in lines consisting of two ranks. Thus they made best use of disciplined volleys to repulse the enemy or unnerve him sufficiently that a bayonet attack could drive him off. Cavalry manoeuvred by squadron, either in line or in column, the troopers wielding their sabres in the charge, but more often than not serving as scouts and baggage escorts; seeking intelligence of the enemy's strength and disposition and guarding the infantry's flanks and rear.

Little can said of their Afghan opponents, for the Amirs maintained no standing force of any kind, relying instead entirely on a large, spontaneously raised force of irregular fighters of varying reliability and effectiveness. They were drawn from the countryside and assembled on the word of a local *mullah* (religious teacher or leader), *sirdar* (tribal commander) or the Amir himself, who in theory could summon up untold thousands of tribesmen when required, though with no established terms of service, and thus rendering their long-term commitment uncertain at best and dubious at worse. They wore no uniform and employed the simplest of tactics, sniping from hillside cover with the *jezail* – a long, hand-crafted musket with distinctive curved stock – or, when seeking to close with their enemy, attacking in great swarms without consideration of formation, cutting and slashing with their long, straight swords and knives. (As many as half a dozen knives at a time were tucked tightly into their waist scarf.)

Afghan tribesmen armed with the famous long-barrelled, hand-made *jezail*, whose extraordinary range enabled the tribesmen during the First Afghan War to pick off enemy troops from beyond the range of the standard-issue British smoothbore muskets.

The fighting

From the start, British military authorities had to tackle the problem of dispatching a major expedition from India across the Sutlej and much further east. The shortest route available to the 'Army of the Indus' lay from Peshawar through the Punjab. Even this route was 400 miles and would require moving the army and its materiel – above all its baggage and guns – through the Khyber and other passes ⬚⬚ slow journey to its ultimate destina⬚⬚⬚⬚ ⬚⬚ney would prov⬚ ⬚⬚⬚⬚ Sikhs, th⬚ the en⬚ perm⬚ The ⬚ far l⬚ the ⬚ thenc⬚ times t⬚ proposed⬚ natural obs⬚ some limited t⬚ first 450 miles, in the ⬚⬚⬚⬚⬚ottomed barges on the Sutlej and Indus rivers. In the event, this was the route chosen by British military planners.

The expedition would comprise approximately 10,000 British and Indian troops in two divisions of differing sizes, with the force from the Bengal presidency consisting of nine infantry regiments, one being a Queen's regiment and the others Company troops: the 13th Foot, the Bengal Europeans and seven regiments Bengal Native Infantry. Five regiments of cavalry would accompany the expedition, one of which was a Queen's regiment – the 16th Lancers – and four of Bengalis. Other units included a troop of horse artillery and two companies of foot artillery, all with European personnel, plus two companies of sappers and miners. The smaller contingent provided by the Bombay

Army consisted of two Queen's regiments of foot – the 2nd and 17th – four regiments of Bombay Native Infantry, the 4th Light Dragoons (a Queen's regiment), two regiments of native cavalry, two companies of foot artillery (all European) and one company of sappers and miners. In addition to these forces, a separate force of 6,000 irregulars was raised in India for Shah Shuja's use, consisting of four regiments of infantry, two regiments of cavalry and a troop of horse artillery, equipped from British magazines and led by British officers.

Lieutenant-General Sir John Keane, commanding the Bombay division, was to move initially by water from Bombay to Sind, there to rendezvous with the Bengal division, led by Major-General Sir Willoughby Cotton, with a further 1,200-mile trek through Baluchistan to Kandahar. The contingent raised for Shah Shuja was to move down the Sutlej and Indus where, with the entire army unified, Keane would assume overall command, with Major-General Sir William Nott leading the Bombay division. Sir William Macnaghten, the newly appointed envoy to Shah Shuja, would accompany the expedition.

Even before the army could advance, the *casus belli* of the war appeared to evaporate, for unexpected news arrived announcing the continued resistance of Herat against Persian forces, not least due to the leadership of Lieutenant Eldred Pottinger, an officer in the EIC who had offered to organize the defence of the place upon finding himself in Herat during an unofficial intelligence-gathering operation in Afghanistan. The Persians, worn out by an unprofitable nine-month siege, and bowing to the diplomatic pressure applied by the Russians, who no longer wished to support this enterprise, raised the siege and withdrew, removing all threat of

Russian expansion in western Afghanistan. Not only that, the Russian ambassador to Tehran, who had played an instrumental part in encouraging the Persians to attack Herat, was recalled by the Tsar, as was Vitkevich from the Afghan capital. Auckland received news concerning Herat in early November 1838. This did not dissuade him from proceeding with his grand expedition, however, for he was determined to oust Dost Mohamed from power, an enterprise supported by the Board of Control, the body in London with responsibility over the affairs of the EIC. The expedition, therefore, would proceed as planned.

On 10 December, the Bengal division left Ferozepore and on 19 February 1839 all forces were on the west bank of the Indus, with the deserts of Baluchistan yet to traverse. The force was enormous, with a massive train of camp followers and baggage animals. The Bengal division comprised 9,500 troops, but a staggering 38,000 camp followers and 30,000 camels, the numbers enlarged by the fact that many officers were accompanied by several – sometimes even dozens – of servants, as was the norm in Indian armies. The vast amount of baggage

consisted not merely of necessities like ammunition, food and fodder, but huge quantities of officers' kit, much of this more appropriate to living in camp rather than in the field. All armies operating in and out of India were famous for their prodigious train of vehicles and equipment, but this was exceptional, with knapsacks, blankets and tons of other stores, especially that most essential of all: water. Very little thought had been given to methods of re-supply, with the army foolishly relying substantially on the purchase of local goods and services through the civilian contractors who accompanied the expedition, as well as by living off the land – a practice which in verdant India had generally sufficed during operations in the past, but could not be applied to much of Afghanistan. The folly of these methods soon came apparent, for the wastes of Baluchistan bore no relation to the productive areas of the Punjab or the Ganges Valley, leaving the men short of

The great fortress at Ghazni, which blocked Sir John Keane's advance on the Afghan capital in 1839. The defenders bricked up all the entrances apart from the Kabul Gate (centre), against which a demolition party placed a large charge of gunpowder.

Routes of the Anglo-Indian invasion during the First Afghan War

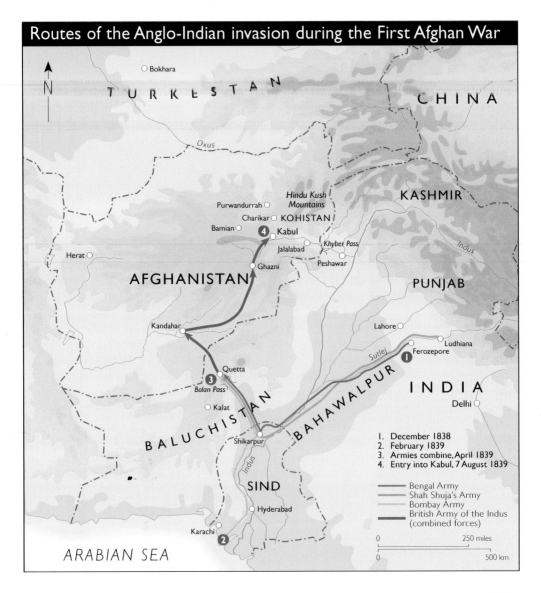

1. December 1838
2. February 1839
3. Armies combine, April 1839
4. Entry into Kabul, 7 August 1839

Bengal Army
Shah Shuja's Army
Bombay Army
British Army of the Indus
(combined forces)

food and water and suffering at the hands of a harsh, unforgiving terrain. Beasts of burden, transport animals and horses suffered especially. Nor was the advance unopposed; hostile tribesmen frequently harassed the column in the Bolan Pass, where any stragglers, especially amongst the camp followers, fell easy victim.

On 31 March 1839, Cotton and Keane's divisions, together with Shah Shuja's contingent, joined at Quetta, but further delay occurred when headquarters failed to consider the most efficient routes, leading to the loss of transport and materiel. The

sufferings of the troops were compounded by inappropriate clothing, for notwithstanding the intense heat, they wore the same heavy leather shakos and scarlet tunics used in Britain. Owing to the weakness of their horses, many troopers had to dismount and move on foot, prodding their animals with their lances. Despite these hardships, the army reached Kandahar on 3 May and oversaw the coronation of Shah Shuja, for whom his people offered only a cool reception. Supplies proved more readily available here, but the army suffered from malaria and dysentery.

While Kabul still remained 325 miles away, the route ahead at least offered more forage and, as the elevation rose, balmier temperatures. Moreover, apart from the harassing attacks by tribesmen in the Bolan, thus far the progress of the army had not been seriously opposed, for Dost Mohamed had blocked the Khyber Pass with his best troops to prevent the Sikhs, should they make the attempt, from advancing on Kabul. He believed the British, with Shuja in Kandahar, would be focusing on operations around Herat. The road to Kabul was not entirely open, however, for having left Nott in Kandahar at the end of June, Keane still faced a gruelling march in summer heat of 200 miles to the north-east to Ghazni, which lay in his path. Ghazni presented walls 70ft high, the whole surrounded by a moat, with a powerful garrison under 21-year-old Hyder Khan, one of Dost Mohamed's sons. Another son led 5,000 Ghilzai cavalry, posted in the hills on either side of the road.

British troops storming the fortress at Ghazni, 23 July 1839. In the absence of a siege train, no alternative remained but to take the place by a *coup de main*. (National Army Museum)

On 20 July, skirmishers from Keane's force scattered the enemy outposts before Ghazni and reconnoitred the fortress, whose walls they discovered to be exceedingly strong – and yet the army's four great siege guns had been left with Nott at Kandahar, and neither mining nor escalade would suffice against walls of such thickness and height. Keane described the place in a letter to Sir Jasper Nicholls, the commander-in-chief in India:

> On the morning of the 21st July the Army in three columns moved close to the outworks of the place, and instead of finding it, as the accounts had stated, very weak and incapable of resistance, a second Gibraltar appeared before us. A high rampart in good repair built on a scarped mound about 35 feet high, flanked by numerous towers, and surrounded by a well constructed [escalade] and a wide wet ditch. In short we were astounded, but there we were.

Intelligence received from Abdul Rashid, a disgruntled nephew of Dost Mohamed, recommended a surprise storm of the Kabul

gate, which rather than being bricked up like the others was merely lightly barred to allow the passage of troops. Keane chose this option, with a diversion or feint directed against the southern face of the fortress. Amidst a night time gale, a contingent of sappers under Captain Peat and Lieutenant Durand quietly approached the walls by traversing a ditch just before daylight on 23 July. Though observed at 150 yards by the defenders and fired upon, the sappers managed to place 75lb bags of powder against the gate and light the cotton fuse. Captain James Douglas, a staff officer with the reserve column, noted:

> The scene at this ... magnificent. T... on both side... and the in... rude walls... a picture ... than any... Suddenly ... thunder, b... artillery; th... the unmistak... air; then the o... illuminated with ... and then the busy musketry went chattering through the streets.

In short, the gate was blown away and a storming party, consisting of four companies of European infantry, rushed the opening. Great confusion initially arose amidst the smoke and noise, for conflicting orders disoriented the troops and prevented the main column from advancing until a bugler from the 13th, refusing to sound the 'Retire', instead blew the 'Advance', causing the infantry to rush forward with bayonets fixed. There followed bitter hand-to-hand fighting in the streets until British and Indian troops prevailed and triumphantly planted the Union Jack on the ramparts of the fortress, whose entire garrison lay dead at a cost to Keane of 200 Anglo-Indian casualties.

The capture of Ghazni led to a number of military developments elsewhere. Dost Mohamed, who during the fighting at Ghazni had 13,000 men nearby but declined to commit them to battle, recalled Akbar Khan and his forces from the Khyber to defend Kabul, and a combined Anglo-Sikh contingent, advancing from Peshawar under General Claude Wade, moved through the pass without encountering resistance. The Amir attempted to gather adherents to his cause to oppose Keane's advance, but none would materialize, for Macnaghten had paid out generous bribes to the chiefs, leaving Dost Mohamed no option but to flee northwards, with Akbar's cavalry in train.

The Army of the Indus entered Kabul on 6 August 1839, with the 60-year-old Shah Shuja arriving the following day on a white charger to take up a throne he had not occupied in three decades. The enterprise had taken ten months, but Auckland's plan had thus far succeeded at relatively little cost to the army, though sickness had taken its toll. With Shah Shuja now in power, Keane returned to India with the Bombay Division and the cavalry, leaving Cotton commanding at Kabul and Nott and a small garrison to occupy Kandahar.

The presence of British troops in Afghanistan was essential, for restoring Shah Shuja to the throne was not sufficient in a turbulent country where he enjoyed virtually no support. Consequently, recognizing the need for a long-term British garrison in the capital, engineers constructed a cantonment on the outskirts of the city in the spring of 1840, with the garrison establishing their lives on the Indian model, enjoying impromptu horse races, sports competitions, amateur theatricals, cricket matches and concerts run by the regimental bands, all to the bemusement of the Afghan populace. With garrison life established on a relatively civilized footing, the families of some officers even made the hazardous journey to join them.

Some of the garrison began to insinuate themselves with the female population of Kabul, thus engendering the hatred of Afghan men, building up resentment in a society where vengeance formed an integral part of tribal life. Burnes was considered by the populace to be the worst offender, with Afghan sensitivities about alcohol also largely trampled upon. Still, the city remained quiet throughout 1840, the monotony only relieved by two developments. First, news arrived in July that the Russians had renewed operations by launching an expedition against the Khan of Khiva, 700 miles to the north-west beyond the Hindu Kush, though this had come to grief in the deserts. Second, on 6 November, after failing to defeat a small force of Indian cavalry, Dost Mohamed appeared unexpectedly in Kabul and surrendered himself to Macnaghten, who sent him into honourable exile in India.

Despite the inefficiency and unpopularity of Shuja's government, the country remained tranquil throughout most of 1841, not least owing to the large subsidies furnished by the Company to tribal chiefs, such as those of the Pathan Ghilzais, who controlled the western approach to the Khyber, to keep them pacified and to maintain open communications and supply lines back to

Encampment of Major-General William Nott's army, fresh from Kandahar, outside Kabul, late September 1842. The city lies beyond the rows of tents, with the fortress of the Bala Hissar on the hillside (left) overlooking the city.

India. But this expedient could not continue indefinitely, for both Britain's new Tory government under Sir Robert Peel and Company officials in Calcutta were growing anxious about the rising costs to the Indian revenue. With an eye for economy, therefore, Macnaghten began to reduce the size of payments – Auckland slashed by over half the £8,000 subsidy he paid annually to the Ghilzais – and ordered the withdrawal back through the Khyber to India of Sir Robert Sale's brigade, which left Kabul en route for Quetta on 10 October. Both measures proved grave mistakes. The Ghilzai chiefs east of Kabul, incensed by the reduction of the subsidy, confronted Sale's force in the narrow defiles of the Khurd-Kabul Pass, obliging the brigade to fight its way through and find refuge in the fort at Jalalabad.

British fortunes now took a turn for the worse. Officers out shooting game found themselves stoned by angry villagers and soldiers were set upon in the streets. In late October an isolated outpost in Kohistan, north of Kabul, held by Shah Shuja's troops under British officers, was destroyed by tribesmen, and on 2 November, a howling mob, angered by his philandering, surrounded Burnes' house in Kabul, set it

on fire and murdered Burnes, his brother and another officer. Strong action on the part of the garrison might have averted further trouble, but Cotton had returned to India for reasons of health a number of months earlier and his successor, Major-General William Elphinstone, was not the stuff of resolution and sound leadership but rather a mere figurehead appointed by Auckland as a cipher likely to carry out Macnaghten's decisions without question. Old, crippled with rheumatic gout, with no field experience since Waterloo and possessed of a courteous manner in a situation that demanded decisiveness and resolution, Elphinstone failed to take action as a result of Burnes' death, while his immediate subordinate, Brigadier-General John Shelton, jealous of his position, allowed events to deteriorate, if only to spite his superior. In a letter that betrayed the very essence of Elphinstone's unsuitability for such an important post in a period of profound crisis, he addressed Macnaghten after Burnes' murder: 'We must see what the

Afghan tribesmen dragging an artillery piece onto the crest of the Bemaru ridge overlooking Kabul, with the Bala Hissar in the middle distance, c. November 1841. The vulnerable position of the British cantonment, immediately below, rendered it indefensible against bombardment.

morning brings and then think what can be done.' In due course Macnaghten ordered Elphinstone to occupy the Bala Hissar, a royal palace and fortress overlooking the city, in an effort to intimidate the population, but the riots continued unabated, and with greater intensity. The crisis deepened when, two days later, a fort containing all the garrison's stores became isolated from the cantonment, which contained only two days' rations.

The situation grew more perilous as tribesmen entered the city to join those of their compatriots who chose to snipe at British and Indian troops, isolated and penned up. With Elphinstone increasingly ill, command devolved upon Shelton who, with most of Kabul now in the hands of the rebels, remained with a small body of troops in the Bala Hissar to defend Shah Shuja. He evacuated the rest, about 6,000, in favour of the cantonment, a rectangular area no larger than 1,000 by 600 yards surrounded by a low rampart and a narrow ditch. The whole cantonment was overlooked by high ground, which the Afghans immediately occupied, dominating it on all sides and rendering the Anglo-Indian force extremely vulnerable and under effective siege. Elphinstone himself had complained in April about the poor state of the city's defences in general and of the

cantonment's in particular, notwithstanding more defensible positions to hand:

> The City is extensive, very dirty & crowded & a great deal of business apparently going on in the Bazar [sic]. It is situated in a hollow, surrounded by high mountains ... The cantonment is ... not very defensible without a number of men, as people can come in from without at many points. This, in the event of troops being requested elsewhere, would be very inconvenient, & I am a good deal puzzled [as to] what is now the best thing to be done.

To make matters worse, Elphinstone constantly interfered with Shelton's command and made a number of poor tactical decisions, including failed attempts to drive off the Afghans; even the 44th Foot, the general's own regiment, refused to obey orders.

The future soon became still more bleak: mobs carried away the garrison's grain and medical stores, inexplicably placed in an old stone fort almost a quarter of a mile outside the perimeter of the cantonment, and thus impossible to protect adequately. Food and fodder were running short, Sale's brigade was five days' march from Kabul at Gandamak and thousands of Ghilzai fighters had flocked to the area, blocking any prospect of the general returning even though he was recalled. Meanwhile, more than 300 miles to the south-west at Kandahar, any attempt by Nott to bring relief would take five weeks of marching – and only so long as the passes were not blocked by snow and his Indian contingent, accustomed to the warmer climates of India, could survive as an effective fighting force while the thermometer continued to descend below freezing.

Thus, with no means of breaking the siege and with circumstances growing increasingly desperate, on 19 November Macnaghten and Elphinstone agreed that the army could not winter in Kabul, and after fighting around the village of Bemaru, in which rebels routed British troops, who fled back to the cantonment, the situation remained unchanged. At the end of the month, hostilities were replaced with negotiations, for the garrison was close to starvation, the horses reduced to gnawing at tent pegs and tree bark, and morale was collapsing, as Lieutenant Vincent Eyre observed: 'Our force resembled a ship in danger of wrecking, for want of an able pilot.' Macnaghten opened talks on 11 December with the Afghans, now led by Akbar Khan, Dost Mohamed's son, fresh from Turkestan. Their unenviable position dominated British thoughts: remain in Kabul and starve – only two days' supply of food remained – or abandon the cantonment without a promise from their opponents of safe passage back to India.

In negotiations conducted on the banks of the Kabul River, the British agreed never to enter Afghanistan again without the express request of the Afghan government, in exchange for immediate provisions and their withdrawing from Kabul on the 15th. The withdrawal would be under safe conduct as far as Ludhiana, on Indian soil – with payments, effectively bribes, made to various tribes in exchange for their non-belligerence during the withdrawal and the neutrality of Akbar Khan.

The Bala Hissar was duly evacuated on the day appointed, leaving Shah Shuja to carry on as best he could, but the main British garrison in the cantonment, complete with its large contingent of dependent women, children, servants and sick, now faced a difficult and dangerous journey, with all the necessary preparation causing delays to departure. Five inches of snow already covered the ground. The British stalled for time, while the Afghans added to the terms already agreed. Macnaghten believed he could divide his enemies with promises of further payments to come, but the Afghans grew suspicious of such a ploy, and at a meeting with Akbar on 23 December to consider new terms for the withdrawal of the army, Macnaghten was killed, and with his death all trust between the two sides evaporated.

Kabul from the viewpoint of the royal palace and fort known as the Bala Hissar. (Author's collection)

On Christmas Day, in return for the British leaving behind the military treasure, carrying with them only six field pieces, and the surrender of hostages in the form of all the married men and their families, Akbar promised safe conduct to Peshawar. Notwithstanding the desperate straits in which he found himself, Elphinstone could not possibly agree to such terms, and thus the army would have to fight its way through the winter snows. 'I fear but few of us will live to reach the provinces whether we go by treaty or not,' Lady Sale, wife of the general, penned in her diary; her anxieties worsened by the widely held view that Elphinstone was utterly incapable of handling affairs. No sooner was an order issued than it was countermanded; his subordinates questioned his commands to the extent that they virtually flouted his authority, and with enemies all around and inadequate leadership within, the whole of the army became demoralized amidst a growing logistical crisis, as supplies dwindled and the temperature continued to fall.

Many members of his staff warned Elphinstone not to undertake what was likely to be a disastrous – as well as a dishonourable – journey, especially Macnaghten, who emphasized how the army would be abandoning massive amounts of government property as well as Shah Shuja himself, whose installation had been the very basis for the army's presence in Afghanistan in the first place. According to Captain George Lawrence, Macnaghten's secretary, Macnaghten had observed that:

> … even if we could make good our retreat, we could carry with us no shelter for the troops, who would in consequence, at this inclement season, suffer immensely, while our camp followers, amounting to many thousands, must inevitably be utterly destroyed. As to any hope of successful negotiations, it appeared to him in vain, so long as there was no party among the insurgents of sufficient strength and influence to insure the fulfilment of any treaty we might enter into.

Against such advice, Elphinstone prevailed. After the Afghans postponed the date of withdrawal with disingenuous excuses that they had yet to accumulate sufficient stocks of supplies for the journey and pleas that an escort had yet to be arranged, Elphinstone ordered the column to move on the morning of 6 January 1842. The advanced guard consisted of the 44th (Queen's) Foot, irregular Indian cavalry units, two 6-pdrs, sappers and miners, mountain artillery and other elements ahead of the main body. The main body itself included the 5th and 37th Native Infantry, the army's treasury, more irregular cavalry, a regiment of loyal Afghan infantry and two 6-pdr guns. The rearguard was composed of the 54th Native Infantry, 5th Native Cavalry, and two 6-pdrs. In total, the force consisted of 690 men of the 44th Foot and the Horse Artillery, 3,800 *sepoys* and *sowars*, 36 British women and children and 12,000 under-nourished, freezing and fear-stricken camp followers, nearly all of them Indians. The sick and wounded could not be

Afghan tribesmen in winter dress, c. 1842, wearing *poshteens*: coats with a leather exterior lined on the inside with fur. These were ideal protection in a land with long, forbidding winters.

transported and were left to their fate – the mercy, such as it was, of the Afghans.

The garrison duly emerged from Kabul into sub-zero temperatures and foot-deep snow, making for the mountains beyond, with 90 miles to traverse until assured safety in Hindustan.

Once the column was underway, order broke down rapidly as the biting cold numbed the trudging figures, the command and staff structure ceased to function and Ghilzai tribesmen constantly harassed the column, killing and plundering with increasing impunity as the troops and followers grew ever more weary and frost-bitten. Without food or fuel, thousands died daily, especially amongst the civilians, whose panic drove them into the ranks of the soldiery, disturbing their order and increasing the sense of despair. Eyre recorded the ghastly spectacle:

Dreary indeed was the scene over which with drooping spirits and dismal forebodings we had to bend our

The retreat from Kabul, 6–13 January 1842

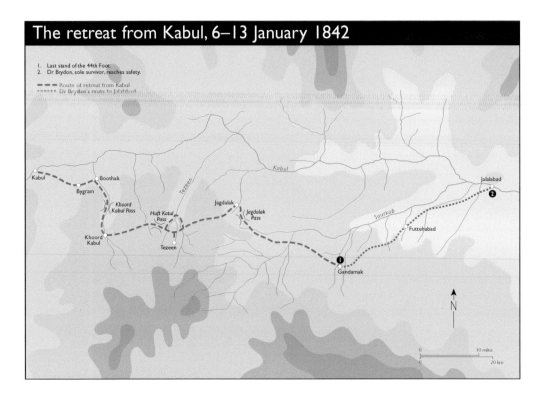

1. Last stand of the 44th Foot.
2. Dr Brydon, sole survivor, reaches safety.

▬ ▬ ▬ Route of retreat from Kabul
▪▪▪▪▪▪ Dr Brydon's route to Jalalabad

unwilling steps. Deep snow covered every inch of mountain and plain with one unspotted sheet of dazzling white, and so intensely bitter was the cold, as to penetrate and defy the defences of the warmest clothing.

Clearly, Akbar's promise of safe conduct had either been a product of subterfuge or a pledge made on the basis of cooperation with tribes who later reneged on their offer. Whatever the case, the army and its dependents were left to run a gauntlet from which it possessed virtually no protection, least of all the civilians. Captain Charles Mackenzie observed a little Indian girl:

It was a beautiful little girl about two years old, just strong enough to sit upright with its little legs doubled under it, its great black eyes dilated to twice their usual size, fixed on the armed men, the passing cavalry and all the strange sights that met its gaze … one of the many innocents [later to be] slaughtered on the road.

Still, on the third day of the retreat the surviving Europeans with wives and children who surrendered themselves to Akbar's protection were not harmed, as agreed. The ambushes and sniping nevertheless continued: the Afghans drove off what was left of the baggage animals and continued to cut down stragglers. On 8 January, having covered only two miles the day before, the miserable straggling column approached the imposing five-mile long Khurd-Kabul Pass. The defile was of such depth as to block out direct sunlight on the icy stream that flowed through its centre. On the heights thousands of fearless Ghilzais assembled to issue a destructive fire. 'They had erected small stone breastworks behind which they lay,' Mackenzie recorded, 'dealing out death with perfect impunity to themselves.' By the time the troops, baggage carts, animals and camp followers had negotiated their way through the pass, 500 soldiers and many times that number of camp followers had perished.

By 10 January, little was left of the original force apart from Elphinstone and his staff, 50 *sowars* of the 5th (Native)

Captain Colin Mackenzie, Madras Army, c. 1842, formerly one of the hostages held in Kabul, wearing native Afghan dress. (National Army Museum)

Cavalry and perhaps 200 men of the Horse Artillery and 44th Foot, which though drastically reduced in number, remained a disciplined force. This moved in single file, or in pairs at best, through the 50-yard Tunghi Taraki Gorge, where the Afghans again lay in ambush. By the time it emerged and reached the village of Tezeen on the afternoon of the 10th, Elphinstone's command was down to a mere 240 Europeans, a handful of *sepoys* and 3,000 of the original 12,000 camp followers.

The remains of the army, mind and body frozen, could do nothing more than simply carry on, struggling through the snows, which apart from the cold offered a further agony. 'My eyes', Captain Johnson complained, 'had become so inflamed from the reflection of the snow that I was nearly blind, and the pain intense.' From Tezeen it was another 20 miles to the two-mile Jagdalak Pass where, as before, tribesmen massed on the heights picked off members of the column, now partially protected by darkness. On the evening of the

Last stand of the 44th (East Essex) Regiment at Gandamak, during the retreat from Kabul to Jalalabad, 13 January 1842. Captain Soulter concealed the regimental colours by wrapping them around his waist beneath his *poshteen*. (National Army Museum)

'The Remnants of an Army', an engraving based on Lady Butler's famous late Victorian oil painting of Dr William Brydon, the only member of the Kabul garrison to reach the fort at Jalalabad, after the destruction of the Army of the Indus in January 1842.

11th, on accepting an invitation from Akbar to discuss the difficulty of enforcing the Ghilzais' agreement to allow the column to proceed unhindered, Elphinstone and Shelton found themselves prisoners.

Meanwhile, the remnants of the Army of the Indus, numbering but 150 men of the 44th, 16 dismounted artillerymen, and 25 troopers of the 5th Light Cavalry, now under Brigadier-General Thomas Anquetil, continued their retreat towards Jalalabad, held by General Sale, with the 44th repulsing the Ghilzais with their bayonets on at least one occasion and slowly negotiating their way towards the end of the Jagdalak Pass. There the track narrowed to not much more than a goat path, blocked by an abbatis through which, after a panic under fire that left Anquetil and many others dead, a few dozen survivors emerged. And thus, on 13 January, the last of the survivors – a huddled group of 20 men of the 44th – made a last stand on a small icy hill near the village of Gandamak, the officers carrying only their swords and pistols, the men their muskets with three or four cartridges apiece. When they had expended their ammunition they fought with bayonet and clubbed musket before falling before the onslaught.

Only a single survivor of this march of death remained: Dr William Brydon, a 30-year-old Scot, an assistant surgeon who with five others had left the Jagdalak Pass at night and taken a route over the hills towards Jalalabad, in the course of which hostile villagers killed his companions and wounded him. On the 13th, exhausted but still mounted atop his bedraggled, dying pony, he approached the fortress at Jalalabad, where he was spotted from a rooftop by a staff officer named Major Henry Havelock, who had distinguished himself in the Burma campaign of 1824-25 and would later do so on a far greater scale during the Indian Mutiny of 1857-58, in which he would play a prominent part as a senior commander. 'As he got nearer,' Havelock recorded of Brydon's slow approach:

… it was distinctly seen that he wore European clothes and was mounted on a travel-hacked yaboo [pony], which he was urging on with all the speed of which it yet remained master. A signal was made to him by someone on the walls, which he answered by waving a private soldier's forage cap over his head. The Caubul gate was then thrown open and several officers, rushing out, received and recognised in the traveller the first, and it is to be feared the last, fugitive of the ill-fated force at Caubul in Dr. Brydon.

How the war ended

With the total destruction of the Army of the Indus, the Anglo-Indian garrison under General Sale at Jalalabad stood perilously isolated, with no immediate prospect of relief and no hope of reaching the safety of India without reinforcement. Brydon's lone appearance forcefully revealed how little Sale – who naturally assumed his wife had perished with the others – could rely on the good faith of the Afghans to permit him an unmolested withdrawal from their soil. He had been holding the fortress of Jalalabad since November 1841 with a force composed of the 13th Foot, the 35th Bengal Native Infantry, a squadron of the 5th Bengal Light Cavalry, a troop of loyal Afghan irregular horse and a small contingent of gunners and sappers. With these he dispersed a local body of tribesmen in the vicinity and then proceeded to repair the fortifications, which

Brigadier-General Sir Robert Sale, defender of Jalalabad. (Author's collection)

lay in decay. Several Afghan attacks followed over the course of November and December, and on 19 December an earthquake happened to hit the area, wrecking much of Sale's work on the defences, but also disrupting his opponents' plans. Then, with the elimination of the Army of the Indus, Akbar Khan arrived in February 1842 to surround the place. Sale had no choice but to remain *in situ*, for he had received word that no relief would arrive from Peshawar for several months.

The siege of Jalalabad has entered the annals of Victorian legend. Sale mounted a spirited defence, launching sorties to interfere with Afghan siege operations, rounding up enemy cattle and collecting critically needed forage to sustain the garrison until relief could arrive. Aid was, in fact, on its way, thanks to the policy of Lord Ellenborough, Auckland's successor as Governor-General of India, in the form of 8,000 men comprising the aptly and grandly named 'Army of Retribution' under Major-General George Pollock, who on 5 April attacked the Afghans holding the Khyber Pass. In this, the first British military experience along this famous route between India and Afghanistan, Pollock did not commit the folly of marching straight through the Pass. Instead, he made a proper study of the place and realized that his only chance of making it through was to command and hold the heights by sending out strong patrols to drive the Afridis off the heights, thereby enabling the slower-moving main body, guns and baggage to negotiate the pass unmolested. Pollock's men took each prominent position one after another, until the route to Jalalabad was open.

During Pollock's advance, marked by bitter hand-to-hand fighting the length of the Tezeen and Jagdalak passes, Lieutenant

John Greenwood recorded his impressions
of one of the more barbarous recorded
incidents in a conflict notorious for
its savagery:

> There is a ferocity about the Afghans
> which they seem to imbibe with their
> mother's milk. A soldier … saw a
> Kyberee boy apparently about six years
> of age with a large knife, which his puny
> arm had scarcely sufficient strength to
> wield, engaged in an attempt to hack off
> the head of a dead sergeant. The young
> urchin was so completely absorbed in
> his savage task, that he heeded not the
> approach of a soldier of the dead man's
> regiment – who coolly took him up
> on his bayonet and threw him over
> the cliff.

In April 1842, upon an unconfirmed report
that Pollock's force was being held back
in the Khyber, Sale decided to launch a
large-scale sortie with a view to supporting
the relief column's advance. When dawn
broke on the 7th, he attacked the Afghan
camp, situated two miles west of the city,
with three columns. Within two hours his
force drove off Akbar's men, captured
his guns, burned his camp and drove in
a flock of 500 sheep and goats, persuading
his opponent to make no further attempts
to harass or seize Jalalabad. On the 16th,
155 days after the siege began, Pollock's
men reached the town, finding instead of
a starving and demoralized garrison, Sale
and his men in high spirits from their
recent success and jocularly welcoming
in the relief force with the 13th Queen's
playing the Scottish tune, 'Eh, but ye've
been lang a' coming'.

Pollock's force had arrived simply to
relieve Jalalabad, for Lord Ellenborough, at
his post since February, strongly wished to
withdraw all British and Indian troops from
Afghanistan once the remaining garrisons
had been rescued. The Army of the Indus
was of course no more and the garrison of
Ghazni had fallen prisoner, but Sale had
been saved and other troops continued to
hold out at Kalat-i-Gilzai, between Kabul
and Kandahar. Withdrawal now had to be
conducted so as to retain as much British

Major-General George Pollock's column meeting
resistance during its advance to the relief of Jalalabad,
5 April 1842.

pride and prestige as possible. While Pollock was relieving Jalalabad, reinforcements were arriving at Kandahar, enabling General Nott in turn to relieve Kalat-i-Gilzai in May. That accomplished, Ellenborough ordered both forces out of Afghanistan, a task that neither commander could achieve until adequate baggage animals were available. Moreover, both generals hoped to remain in the country until such time as the Afghans could be best _____ eir capital once aga_____s, for an unk_____rs and vari_____n _____ ge_____ Po_____ N_____ In_____ rou_____ wrea_____ he cho_____

With Sa_____ ___s division, Pollock left Jalalabad on 20 August and on 8 September reached the site of the 44th's last stand at Gandamak, a scene eerily described in Greenwood's diary:

The top of the hill was thickly strewed with the bodies of the slain. Some were mere skeletons, whilst others were in better preservation. Their hair was still on their heads, and their features were perfect, although discoloured … a vulture which had been banqueting on them hopped carelessly away to a little distance, lazily flapping his huge wings … As the foul bird gazed listlessly at me, I almost fancied him the genius of destruction gloating over his prey.

Akbar disputed his advance at the Jagdalak and Tezeen passes, but Pollock's experience in mountain fighting held his force in good stead, and he advanced with minimal casualties while exacting a heavy toll on the Afghans, whose attacks dried up before they withdrew northwards, abandoning the route to Kabul. As Anglo-Indian forces advanced unopposed through the Khurd-Kabul Pass,

they encountered the skeletal remains of more of Elphinstone's column, many still wearing the tattered remnants of their uniforms. 'I shall never forget the sight I saw here,' Greenwood recorded. 'The poor fellows who had fallen in Elphinstone's retreat, lay together in heaps. Their bodies absolutely choked up the narrow pass, and our men were marching amid a mass of human corruption.'

Nott divided his force, with one contingent retiring through Baluchistan to Sind, and the other under himself beginning its advance from Kandahar on 10 August. His troops sharply defeated the Afghans at Ghazni having, like Pollock, occupied the heights in the wake of the main body and swept away the bands of tribesmen on either side of the line of march. Again like Pollock's column, Nott's force also passed over much of the area still bearing evidence of the remains of Elphinstone's ill-fated column. They encountered the identical spectacles of horror and the folly that can follow poor military decision-making: human skeletons; the remains of thousands of bullocks, horses and camels, their bones long since picked clean by vultures and wolves; broken-down artillery, abandoned carts and wagons; and the other detritus of war.

On reaching Kabul on 15 September, Pollock established his camp on the site of a racecourse originally constructed by Elphinstone's men before the revolt. Nott's force arrived two days later, and with the Union Jack once again flying over the Bala Hissar it now remained to decide what course to take, the Afghan chiefs fearing widescale retribution. Pollock ordered the destruction of the Char Chowk bazaar in reprisal for Macnaghten's murder and the public display of his mutilated body, while Sale led a punitive expedition into Kohistan, where he burned down the towns of Istalif and Charikar. The hostages and most of the handful of prisoners taken during the retreat were miraculously still alive – apart from Elphinstone, who had died in captivity from dysentery – and the Afghans released them unharmed. Shah Shuja had been murdered the previous April, his son having taken his place, but Akbar, chastened though still in the field, continued to pose a military threat. Shuja was to be left to his own devices, for Pollock had orders not to interfere in political matters, a new policy of non-intervention in Afghan politics was issued in the form of Ellenborough's proclamation of 1 October 1842:

> Disasters unparalleled in their extent unless by the errors in which they originated, and by the treachery by which they were completed have, in one short campaign, been avenged … The British arms now in possession of Afghanistan will now be withdrawn to the [River] Sutlej [in the Punjab]. The Governor-General will leave it to the Afghans themselves to create a government amidst the anarchy which is the consequence of their crimes.

On 12 October, having laid waste to most of the city apart from the Bala Hissar, the Army of Retribution left Kabul en route to Peshawar. Apart from several attacks conducted in the passes against the rearguard under Nott, Anglo-Indian forces encountered no formal opposition to their withdrawal from Afghanistan, and on 23 December Pollock's combined army finally reached India at Ferozepore.

Florentia, Lady Sale (1787–1853)

Florentia, Lady Sale, heroine of the retreat from Kabul in 1842 and her subsequent period of captivity, was the wife of Major-General Robert Sale, who it will be recalled had been sent back to India from Kabul, only to find himself forced to take refuge in the fort at Jalalabad en route. Having decided to remain behind with the garrison still controlling the Afghan capital, Lady Sale became an unwitting participant in one of the greatest catastrophes in British military history, during which time she witnessed the destruction of the Army of the Indus and endured a period of harsh captivity. Yet throughout this ordeal she maintained an invaluable account of her experience,

Florentia, Lady Sale, the indomitable wife of Major-General Sir Robert Sale. By choosing to remain with the Kabul garrison after the departure of her husband for Jalalabad, she later found herself an unwitting participant in the fateful retreat of January 1842. Her memoirs number amongst many excellent reminiscences of the First Afghan War.

and was one of the few surviving witnesses of a tragedy that left virtually every other participant dead along snow-driven mountain paths, in the deep gorges of the Khurd-Kabul Pass and on the body-strewn summit of the hill at Gandamak.

It will be recalled that Elphinstone's demoralized, exhausted army left Kabul on 6 January 1842. In all, Anglo-Indian forces numbered 4,500 troops and 12,000 camp followers, many of the latter being soldiers' wives and children, but mostly Indian retainers, servants, merchants and their families. The day was clear and frosty, with nearly a foot of snow already on the ground. Terms for the safe conduct of the column as far as Peshawar had been made with the *sirdars* and Mohamed Akbar Khan at the extortionate cost of 14 and a half *lakhs*.

The column began to move at 9.30am on 6 January with no molestation of the advance guard, as 50–100 Afghans milling about the gates of the cantonment watched the scene. Lady Sale rode near the head of the column, together with other prominent civilians, mostly officers' wives and children. Progress was very slow and the first mile was only covered in two and a half hours. The bullocks found great difficulty in dragging the gun carriages through the snow and much of the column lumbered through the bottleneck created by a narrow, makeshift bridge constructed the night before over the Kabul River, although reconnaissance had already determined it was easily fordable nearby, albeit only to those prepared to brave the freezing water. A great deal of baggage and commissariat supplies was left behind in the struggle to cross this first obstacle – just one characteristic of the travails yet in store.

The troops themselves had been on half rations during the whole period of the siege, with even less for camp followers, while the cattle – notwithstanding a recent supply of barley – had long subsisted on twigs and bark, leaving them fatally weakened in freezing conditions. In any event, they were fated never to reach their destination, for the poorest and hungriest camp followers rapidly devoured those animals that collapsed from starvation. Apart from the desperate shortage of food, both soldiers and civilians suffered from a total absence of firewood, forcing them to burn everything combustible: boxes, chests of drawers and all manner of furniture still in their possession, apart from the waggons themselves. Indeed, Lady Sale's last dinner and breakfast at Kabul had been cooked with the wood of a mahogany dining table.

When the rearguard finally left the cantonment, the Afghans immediately began to occupy the buildings and fire upon the last party to depart. This caused panic amongst the servants, who cast aside their loads and ran off, so abandoning much of the privately carried baggage, the commissariat and ammunition at the very outset of the retreat. Before the day was even out men, women and children – an appalling assortment of the sick, dead and dying – began to litter the roads, deprived of the will to persevere and resigned to their fate. Their bodies encumbered the passage of others, all numbed by the intense cold and ignorant of the other foe yet to appear. That night, in the complete absence of tents – much less any proper protection from the elements – an officer managed to pitch a makeshift covering over Lady Sale and a few of her companions, providing the barest of comfort as the wind blew in under the sides to attack the occupants, stiff and huddled in their *poshteens* (a sheepskin jacket with a fleece lining). By the end of the first day, Lady Sale had only travelled six miles but hundreds of civilians and some of the troops had already fallen by the wayside, the army had abandoned two horse artillery pieces on the road, and, ominously, all of the Shah Shuja's troops had now deserted.

So ponderous proved the journey and so strung-out had the column become, that

on the morning of the 7th the rearguard only reached the main body at 2.00am, with stragglers making enquiries as to the whereabouts of their units. With the breakdown of unit cohesion came the decline of morale, with a sense of forlorn inevitability reinforced as the growing light revealed the frozen corpses of those who had succumbed during the night. Lady Sale, still in the advance guard, moved off at 7.30am without the troops receiving so much as an order to proceed or a bugle sounding. As discipline among the *sepoys* began to collapse, some wandered ahead of the advance guard. Others could not locate their units and cast away their weapons to lighten the load, while some, too injured or too weak failed to keep up, resigning themselves to certain death. No sooner was baggage left behind than Afghans began to appear and plunder it. The early signs of this form of depredation were already evident in the fact that the cantonment was looted and burned shortly after its evacuation; the fate of the wounded left behind can only be surmised.

Lady Sale on horseback during the retreat.

But worse now followed, with the first serious attacks on the column beginning on the 7th – only the second day of the retreat – when a force of screaming Afghans sallied out of a small fort and briefly captured two pieces of artillery; which when retaken after a stiff fight were abandoned, the guns spiked by the officers to render them inoperable. As the column advanced, the Afghans grew in numbers along its flanks and increasingly harassed its centre and rear, the camp followers suffering the most, as Lady Sale recorded: 'Numbers of unfortunates have dropped, benumbed with cold, to be massacred by the enemy.' After marching five miles since morning, the column halted before the opening of the Khurd-Kabul Pass. Lady Sale was exceedingly disconcerted by the stoppage, for she knew the troops possessed only five and a half days' rations with which to reach Jalalabad, and the animals could not forage on account of the snow on the ground, which was more than a foot deep. The senior officers squabbled over whether to camp or push on, before finally agreeing on the latter course, and by the time they reached Bhoodkhak there was scarcely any baggage remaining of any kind. Two more 6-pdrs were abandoned,

since the horses could no longer pull them, leaving only two serviceable guns remaining and almost no ammunition – much of which had already been abandoned through ineptitude, carelessness and lack of animal transport. By the end of the second day, Lady Sale observed the *sepoys* mixing with the camp followers, with no hope of reforming themselves into their respective units. In any event, they had suffered such grievous losses from death and desertion that their unit designations bore little relation to reality. Even with snow in abundance, water was not easily obtained, for there was no firewood with which to melt it, and those who sought to gather water from streams still unfrozen were fired on by tribesmen.

By 8 January an already dire situation had utterly degenerated, with an atmosphere of

The third day of the retreat from Kabul, 8 January 1842. Emboldened by the inability of Anglo-Indian troops properly to defend themselves and by the helplessness of the camp followers, Afghan tribesmen snipe from elevated positions and make forays directly against the column, seizing Captain and Mrs Anderson's young daughter (left) and fatally wounding Lieutenant Sturt (right), son-in-law to Lady Sale (mounted, centre background), with General Elphinstone to her front. Along the hillside (right) soldiers of the 44th fruitlessly attempt to disperse the harassing Ghilzais.

foreboding in the air. 'At sunrise,' Lady Sale observed, 'no order had been issued for the march, and the confusion was fearful. The force was perfectly disorganized, nearly every man paralysed with cold, so as to be scarcely able to hold his musket or move. Many frozen corpses lay on the ground.' Some of the *sepoys* still with the ranks – or in any event still on their feet – took the futile and fatal decision to burn their caps and clothes for the modicum of fleeting warmth this act of desperation provided. But the increasing forays by the Afghans caused the greatest distress, and when a force of tribesmen attacked the rear of the column a panic ensued, the camp followers rushing to the front for protection from the troops, although many soldiers were no longer even under arms. The Afghans continued to gather in greater and greater numbers, harassing the column from the heights with their long, accurate *jezails*. 'Bullets kept whizzing by us, as we sat on our horses, for hours,' Lady Sale recorded, the 44th and 37th Native Infantry returning fire as best they could against a virtually unseen enemy perched amongst the rocks and precipices high above them.

Eventually, negotiations began between Elphinstone, his officers and Akbar Khan, who agreed to guarantee the column's safe advance across the border, but with the stakes raised: further payment and the surrender of three senior British officers to be detained as hostages as the price for General Sale's evacuation of Jalalabad and withdrawal into Indian territory. These terms were a blatant form of blackmail from those who had already violated the original terms of the agreement, but Elphinstone believed he had no choice but to accept. A handful of officers remained behind as hostages and the march resumed about midday, Lady Sale describing the troops as 'in the greatest state of disorganization: the baggage was mixed in with the advance guard; and the camp followers all pushed ahead in their precipitate flights towards Hindostan'.

No sooner had they advanced half a mile when the Afghans opened a heavy fire on

them, wounding several people and horses in the advance guard, including Sale, her arm struck by a musket ball. Three other musket balls passed through her *poshteen* near the shoulder, but without causing injury. The principal attack, however, struck the main body of the column, what remained of the baggage train, and the rearguard, with a number of civilians, including children, being abducted or killed. Sale described the harrowing experience of many of her civilian compatriots, among them a certain Mrs Mainwaring, an officer's wife with the most precious of burdens:

> She not only had to walk a considerable distance with her child in her arms through the deep snow, but had also to pick her way over the bodies of the dead, dying, and wounded, both men and cattle, and constantly to cross the streams of water, wet up to the knees, pushed and shoved about by men and animals, the enemy keeping up a sharp fire, and several persons being killed close to her.

Two regiments, the 44th and 37th Native Infantry, protected the rear, but as they approached the Khurd-Kabul Pass the Afghans increased their fire from amongst the rocks. The number of wretched soldiers opposing them continued to dwindle, and those that survived, their hands swaddled in gloves and cloth, were barely able to load their weapons, much less manipulate the trigger. To compound the column's predicament, progress ceased for several hours:

> Owing to a halt having taken place in front, the pass was completely choked up; and for a considerable time the 44th were stationary under a heavy fire, and were fast expending their ammunition. The 37th continued slowly moving on without firing a shot, being paralysed with cold to such a degree that no amount of persuasion by their officers could induce them to make any effort to dislodge the enemy, who took from

some of them not only their firelocks,
but even the clothes from their persons.

Eventually, the column halted, some
of the soldiers still determined to hold
onto the one remaining artillery piece by
manhandling it without the aid of horses,
whose strength could not sustain such a
laborious enterprise over broken ground deep
in snow. Other means of defence stood in an
equally parlous state. When the army had left
Kabul, Lady Sale reckoned that each *sepoy*
carried 40 rounds of musket ammunition in
his pouch and 100 spares. Now, only the third
day into the retreat, just three ammunition-
bearing camels remained in the column, with
many *sepoys* possessing not a single cartridge
and no system of distribution in place.
The commissariat had ceased to function,
regimental integrity had in many cases broken
down, desertion was rife, discipline and
morale stood at breaking point, and the scenes
of suffering continued in unremitting fashion:

> It would be impossible for me to
> describe the feelings with which we
> pursued our way through the dreadful
> scenes that awaited us. The road covered
> with awfully mangled bodies, all naked:
> fifty-eight Europeans were counted ...
> the natives innumerable. Numbers of
> the camp followers were still alive, frost
> bitten and starving, some perfectly out
> of their senses and idiotic ... The sight
> was dreadful, the smell of blood
> sickening, and the corpses lay so thick
> it was impossible to look from them,
> as it required care to guide my horse
> so as not to tread upon the bodies.

During the evening of the 8th, Lady Sale
took stock of the disaster, estimating that
500 troops and about 2,500 camp followers
had died from exhaustion, cold or
starvation, or fallen at the hands of the
Afghans. With the prospect of reaching
Jalalabad growing ever more unlikely, she lay
down to sleep in the bitter cold, wrapped as
before in her *poshteen* and sharing a
cramped space with those officers and their
wives who had thus far mercifully survived
an ordeal of catastrophic proportions.

The approach to Jagdalak, 8 September 1842.

Rising on the morning of the 9th, she discovered that many of the soldiers had already moved off, together with a large body of camp followers. 'More than one half of the force is now frostbitten or wounded,' she recorded in her journal, 'and most of the men can scarcely put a foot to the ground. This is the fourth day that our cattle have had no food; and the men are starved with cold and hunger.' Amidst this deepening crisis, a *sirdar* rode out to British headquarters suggesting that the three senior officers, Pottinger, Mackenzie and Lawrence, approach the Afghan garrison of the Khurd-Kabul fort and request protection for the wives and children, guaranteeing their safe escort to Peshawar at a later date. Barring this expedient, there seemed no possibility of their survival. General Elphinstone, now too ill to continue in command, agreed to this proposal, 'in the twofold hope,' Lady Sale surmised:

> ... of placing the ladies and children beyond the dangers and dreadful privations of the camp, and also of showing the *sirdar* that he was sincere in his wish to negotiate a truce, and thus win from him a similar feeling of confidence. Overwhelmed with domestic affliction, neither Mrs Sturt [her

companion, whose husband had just died of his wounds] nor I were in a fit state to decide for ourselves whether we would accept the *sirdar*'s protection or not. There was but faint hope of our ever getting safe to Jellalabad; and we followed the stream.

The women and children, together with their surviving husbands and others, were guided by a circuitous route to the fort where Lady Sale found Akbar Khan and the hostages, together with the civilians taken prisoner over the preceding days. Here began a lengthy period of imprisonment, during which time most of the captives, apart from Elphinstone (whose death almost certainly saved him from disgrace before a court martial) survived the primitive conditions to be rescued later that year when, as we have seen, British military operations resumed.

Lady Sale's husband died three years later at the battle of Mudki, during the war in Sind, a stretch of wild country bordering south-west Afghanistan, leaving his widow with a special pension from the Queen. When Lady Sale herself died at Cape Town on 6 July 1853, the inscription on the simple granite obelisk over her grave summed up her character perfectly: 'Underneath this stone reposes all that could die of Lady Sale.'

Afghanistan: the playground of the Great Game

Dramatic geography dominates Afghanistan and helps explain its role in Britain's strategy for the defence of India, its greatest colonial possession. At the northern end of the subcontinent, the Himalayas run for 1,900 miles, dividing Afghanistan and India from Tibet and China. For the whole of the 19th century, these mountains provided India with a secure front against invasion. For those concerned with the defence of India, the main issue was the security problems posed by the north-western frontier with Afghanistan. Specifically, stretching for 600 miles to the border with Persia sits the formidable Hindu Kush, consisting of a massive chain of mountains, some rising more than 20,000ft, rendering access to and from Central Asia not impossible, but certainly no simple affair. Most of this region was completely unexplored by Europeans in the 19th century, but the passes

that penetrated this forbidding region were known, and where the eastern Hindu Kush connects with the central Hindu Kush, several routes provided access into Afghan Turkestan, which meant that as Russia slowly but inexorably expanded southwards, the Hindu Kush remained the only principal barrier to Afghanistan. Any foreign force that penetrated beyond this chain of mountains would still face the eastern Hindu Kush, whose ridges extended southward into Waziristan and Baluchistan, nearly as far as the Arabian Sea. They provided an uninterrupted natural barrier between India and Afghanistan, with the Indus River flowing roughly parallel, to the east, serving as a metaphorical moat to this fortress wall.

Afghan chiefs and some of their sons during the Second Afghan War.

To the east of the Indus lay areas of considerable settlement. To the west, much more sparsely populated and with an ill-defined border, lay the tribal territories; partly in British India and partly in Afghanistan, in reality neither the British authorities nor Kabul had more than a very limited juristiction over them. Volumes can be written about Afghanistan's vast and varied geography, but for the purposes of this study it was in the eastern area – through which access to and from India was possible – that the strategic issues connected with the Anglo-Afghan Wars were central. For it was this region, stretching from the Bolan Pass in the south to the Khyber Pass in the north – with other, less significant routes in between – that connected eastern Afghanistan with western India.

Afghanistan's three chief cities were, and continue to be, Kabul, Kandahar and Herat. Herat sits at the western end of the Hindu Kush, near the frontier with Persia, present-day Iran. Situated as it is in a fertile region, Herat served as the principal route of advance into Afghanistan from its western

The Jagdalak Pass during the First Afghan War.
(Author's collection)

neighbour and thus, if moving in the opposite direction, as one of the two main avenues for progress into Central Asia. An invasion from the west obviated the need for an attacking force to cross the dreaded Hindu Kush, and once in control of the city an invader possessed not only shelter for his troops against a harsh climate, but a fortified city, ample food for his army and plenty of fodder from the surrounding fertile countryside for his horses and beasts of burden. Thus for centuries Herat served as an important strategic objective for all invading forces and a focus of intense interest to the British government in India, who under no circumstances would accept its occupation by Persian or Russian troops.

Kabul's importance, not merely as the capital city, lay with its position at the crossroads of two important avenues of communication: a road leading through the Hindu Kush into Turkestan and penetrating further into Central Asia, and a mountainous route to Peshawar, in the British Punjab, and beyond to India's northern plains. A third major means of communication across Afghanistan ran from Kabul to Kandahar, moving south-westwards through Ghazni, which controls the second main avenue

into India – through the vital Bolan Pass. Kandahar, like Kabul, is situated at the confluence of two important communications routes of strategic significance – the Herat to Kabul road, and that which connected Herat

Entrance to the Bolan Pass from Dadur, 1842. (National Army Museum)

to Sind (annexed after conquest by British India in 1843) via the Bolan Pass. Since Herat,

The Chunari Pass through the Khurd-Kabul Range. Precipitous mountains and narrow defiles such as these depicted here made Afghanistan an extremely challenging environment in which to prosecute military operations, especially in the depths of winter or the scorching heat of summer. (Author's collection)

Kandahar and Kabul were connected to one another by roads that constituted the principal arteries of communication across the country, it is perhaps understandable that British authorities in India should have regarded the Hindu Kush as the best barrier of defence in the north-west. The further the Russians could be kept at bay beyond this formidable barrier, the better the state of security for India. Failure to keep Russian penetration at bay, especially as far as Kabul or Kandahar, would allow them to influence – and possibly even encourage to hostility – the frontier tribes, against which no natural barrier existed to separate them from the remainder of India.

Thus Afghan geography and the peculiar distribution of its people well into British territory played an important role in encouraging Anglo-Indian intervention. Indeed, nothing less than the threat, real or perceived, to the Indian subcontinent could have inspired military operations in so forbidding an environment. The climate featured extremes of temperature, with winters bringing snow and sub-zero blasts of piercing winds, followed by a rapidly approaching spring that in turn quickly gave way to burning summer temperatures – rising to 110°F and above by June, complete with dust-storms and long absences of rainfall. Add to this a seemingly endless series of rock-strewn hills, narrow defiles, a bleak and waterless terrain, a determined enemy making use of topography ideally suited to ambush and extended defence, and the British had the ingredients of a protracted and costly conflict.

In a country of severe geography and climate, where life is arduous, it is scarcely surprising that the country bred a tough people, influenced as much by Islam as by weather and terrain. The label 'Afghanistan', which literally means 'Land of the Afghans', can only be properly applied to that state from 1747, and largely stands as a 19th-century means for describing more of an ill-defined geographical area than an actual unified political entity. Nor, to be strictly accurate, does the term 'Afghan' apply only to those peoples living within the borders of the country called Afghanistan, for they also include the Pathans living in what was then India in the region stretching from the Swat Valley in the north to Waziristan in the south. In addition to these, the Afghans are divided into two large tribal confederations known as the Duranis and the Ghilzais, the former of whom came to prominence in the mid-18th century when they seized control of the country after the death of the Emperor of Persia, Nadir Shah. The Duranis were and still are best associated with the areas around Kabul, Jalalabad and Herat, whereas their principal rivals, the Ghilzais, who had ruled much of the south of the country prior to the Durani ascendancy, live mostly to the east of a line drawn from Kabul to Kalat-i-Ghilzai. The Ghilzais for the most part lived nomadically, spending their winters on the plains and shifting to the central highlands in the summer months, with large numbers travelling into India via the various passes for purposes of trading and allowing their flocks to graze.

The tribes on the North-West Frontier, under British control after the defeat of the Sikhs in 1849, were also ethnic Afghans. They consisted of peoples related to both the Duranis and Ghilzais, sharing between them a common language in variant forms as either Pashtu or Paktu (though Dari and a host of other languages are also spoken throughout the country), with geography playing some part in their classification – a distinction is made between those living in the plains and those making their homes in the hills and mountains. The Duranis and Ghilzais belong in the former category, together with various other tribes who inhabit the plain around Peshawar and the valleys further north. Those tribes situated in the more rural areas along the eastern border of Afghanistan – straddling both sides, in fact – occupy what is now called the 'tribal territory' or 'tribal lands' that extend from Swat in the north to the towns of Sibi and Pishin in the south. The area runs along much of the length of what was the Afghan–British India border, now in modern Pakistan. These peoples are ethnically diverse, and include the Orakzais, Mahsuds, Mohmands, Afridis, Wazirs and others, many of whom played key parts in the numerous minor campaigns and punitive expeditions fought by British and Indian troops for half a century after the Second Afghan War.

However diverse ethnically and linguistically, Afghans share much in common with one another, placing a high

value on family loyalty and closeness,
personal honour, hospitality, fierce
independence and physical courage.
As such, loyalty to family and tribe or clan
stands above loyalty to the state. On the
other hand, with this heightened sense
of independence comes unreliability and
fickleness. Similarly, the emphasis on
personal honour, while a virtue unto itself,
can manifest itself in a drawn-out personal
campaign of vengeance, with blood-letting
a common and accepted means of satisfying
that need. Moreover, the obsession – from
the Western perspective – with physical
courage can manifest itself in the acts
of aggression and violence that play so
prominent a part in Afghan life. And while
hospitality, whether extended to friends,
strangers or even enemies, is pivotal to
Afghan customs and mores, it possesses
its own limitations; thus, as a consequence
of insult or offence, former guests of
a household may at a stroke become
re-classified as foes according to the
carefully established conventions laid
down by generations of tradition.

Of the approximately four million Afghans
populating the country in the last quarter
of the 19th century, the largest group after
the Duranis and Ghilzais were the Tajiks, a
farming people, although a minority sustained
themselves as shopkeepers and artisans.
The Tajiks lived principally around Herat and
Kabul, and further north in a band of territory
stretching into Turkestan north of the central
highlands. The dominant people of the central
highlands and immediately to the west of
Kabul were the Hazaras, also Persian-speaking,
but of Turkish or Mongol descent, and again
largely an agricultural people. In contrast to
most Afghans, who are Sunni Muslims, the
Hazaras were Shi'ites, a fact that contributed
to their isolation from other tribes.

Across much of the country lived various
nomadic peoples who by definition never
coalesced into an organized, cohesive whole,
as well as various other non-nomadic peoples
too numerous to mention. The heterogeneous
nature of the country militated against any
unified system of defence against British
invasion and yet, conversely, rendered an
invasion of Afghanistan extremely
problematical, with rival groups normally at
each other's throats temporarily united in
resisting a foreign foe.

Not surprisingly, while control over the
nation ostensibly lay with the Amir in Kabul,
the vast extent of the country and the
primitive nature of communication,
combined with the stronger, more localized
allegiances, resulted in the exercise of a sort
of nominal, quasi-rule from the capital at
best and, at worst, complete independence
enjoyed by the more remote peoples. This
accounted for the endemic and chronic
instability so characteristic of Afghan
politics. Nevertheless, a degree of central
control could be applied, and state revenue
was raised, not only through links with the
tribal system, but through the network of
feudal obligations that entitled a chief, or
sirdar (elected from the leading family of the
tribe and holding his post for life), to
command the strict loyalty of his people. In
turn, the *sirdar* often was the recipient of
lands granted by the Amir in exchange for
his service, usually taking the form of levies
of armed men to be furnished during periods
of hostility. Thus, even where no standing
army existed, as during the First Afghan War,
the Amir could raise substantial numbers of
fighters – unquestionably brave and strongly
motivated by religious fervour and
xenophobia, but often indisciplined to boot.

Such, in very brief terms, stood this most
formidable land and people.

Attack on the Peiwar Kotal by the 5th Gurkha
Rifles and 72nd Highlanders, 2 December 1878.
The Gurkhas advance with *yatagan* bayonets fixed to
their Sniders while the Highlander in the foreground
carries the newer Martini-Henry rifle. (National
Army Museum)

PART II

The Second Anglo-Afghan War, 1878–81

Origins and background of the war

By the 1860s, with its defeat at the hands of Britain, France and Turkey in the Crimean War (1853–56) now squarely behind it, Russia was free to continue expansion in Central Asia. The potential threat to British India was used as a possible bargaining chip in negotiations over such questions as naval access through the Bosphorus and Dardanelles, a point denied them under the Treaty of Paris of 1856. Even if the Russians never seriously contemplated an invasion of India – and no strong evidence for this exists – there remained the possibility of a Russian-inspired revolt along the North-West Frontier and within India itself: the same spectre that had inspired Britain to war in 1839 and which would continue to exercise successive governments, the Press and the public alike for the remainder of the 19th century.

When the Crimean War ended the Russian threat to Afghanistan – and, by extension – to India, was minimal. Indeed, a thousand miles separated Peshawar from the closest Russian outposts in Central Asia, situated at the northern ends of the Caspian and the Aral Seas. Lying between British and Russian possessions stood barren plains, desert wastes, the Hindu Kush and other formidable natural obstacles, not to mention various khanates who would contest any Russian penetration into their domains. Nevertheless, from the 1860s the Russians began a cautious advance down the line of the Sir-Darya River from the Aral Sea, justified in 1864 by the Russian Foreign Minister, Prince Gorchakov, as necessary to subdue hostile tribes on the Empire's southern frontiers. This advance led to the capture of Tashkent in 1865 and the creation of a new province, Turkestan, with a new governor, General Konstantin Kauffmann, who was not inclined to slow his country's seemingly irresistible advance southwards.

Within three years he had imposed a treaty on the Amir of Bokhara by which Samarkand fell under Russian control and free passage was obtained through that state. Further to the west, the Russians built a base at Krasnovodsk on the eastern shores of the Caspian, squeezing Khiva between their possessions on both sides. Predictably, the Russians took the city, in 1873, with Khokand following three years later, to be converted into a new province by the name of Fergana. Thus, in less than two decades the distance between Russia's Central Asian possessions and British India had decreased from 1,000 miles to a mere 400 miles, inspiring the new governor of Fergana, General Mikhail Skobolev, to go so far as to propose to his superiors in St Petersburg a three-pronged invasion of India originating from Krasnovodsk, Samarkand and Kashgar.

Quite naturally, Russia's gradual advances south through Central Asia did not go unnoticed by British authorities either in London or Calcutta. As early as the 1860s, John Jacob, Commissioner for Sind (a region annexed to British India by force in 1843), had suggested a permanent British presence in Quetta, beyond the Bolan Pass, enabling troops to threaten the flank and rear of an enemy seeking to enter the Khyber Pass. Yet this advice went ignored until 1876. Some in the Indian government suggested the establishment of a limited protectorate status for Afghanistan, which since the death of Dost Mohamed in 1863 had been ruled by his son, Sher Ali Khan. Such a scheme would enable British troops to control Kandahar and Herat. But this did not appeal to successive governments in London, which preferred to negotiate with Russia rather than confront it, for there was much to be commended in an understanding by which both nations' Asian possessions were

The advance guard of the Anglo-Indian army on the frontier with Afghanistan, November 1878. (Author's collection)

separated from one another by neutral buffer states. In any event, an agreement of 1873 seemed destined to satisfy both parties by recognizing Afghanistan as falling within Britain's sphere of influence, with Russia enjoying the same status respecting Bokhara.

A change of ministry in London in 1874, however, altered matters. Benjamin Disraeli, leading the new Conservative government, eyed Russian advances in Central Asia with considerably more suspicion than his predecessors. His new Secretary of State for India, Lord Salisbury, while not anticipating a Russian invasion, also remained anxious about indirect influence, specifically with respect to Afghanistan. Salisbury appointed Lord Lytton as Viceroy of India (the new designation for the former post of Governor-General, which was abolished immediately after the Mutiny along with the EIC), instructing him to keep Sher Ali clear of Russian influence. Lytton, perceiving danger where none existed, determined that the key to keeping the Russians at bay lay in holding the Hindu Kush or even the line of the Oxus River – a fantastic notion that required more than keeping a watchful eye over Sher Ali's intentions, but controlling him outright. When the Amir politely declined Lytton's overtures for the establishment of close relations with British India, officials in Calcutta felt all the more strongly persuaded that force of arms might be required to prevent the Russians from obtaining some sort of foothold in Afghanistan.

Anglo-Russian tensions were heightened in 1877 by the Russo-Turkish War. During that conflict, the Tsar's troops made considerable progress in their march on Constantinople, whose capture would provide the Russians with unrestricted access to the eastern Mediterranean – the principal cause of the Crimean War, and now more sensitive still for British interests since the opening of the Suez Canal in 1869. Britain had not gone to war with Russia 20 years before to protect Turkey only to see Constantinople fall to the Tsar's forces and the Mediterranean opened to the Russian Black Sea Fleet. Nor was the Russian threat pure fantasy: a division of 15,000 troops established itself in the area between the Oxus and the Hindu Kush. Yet there were in fact no plans to drive into Afghanistan, and the Tsar could not have deployed substantial numbers of troops in the country while simultaneously engaging the Turks hundreds of miles to the west. Nevertheless, with Russian intentions uncertain and the fall of Constantinople possible if not imminent, Disraeli dispatched a fleet to the Dardanelles and troops to Malta.

Unlike the Russo-Turkish conflict that began in 1853 and widened to include Britain and France, the Russo-Turkish War of 1877–78 did not draw in other belligerents. However, when Russia, profiting by its successes in the field, sought to negotiate terms with Turkey from a position of considerable strength, Britain and various other Great Powers threatened war to redress the balance unless Russia agreed to negotiate more lenient terms with the Ottomans. The Congress of Berlin, convened in mid-1878, brought an end to the crisis and obliged

Afghanistan and the North-West Frontier in the 19th century

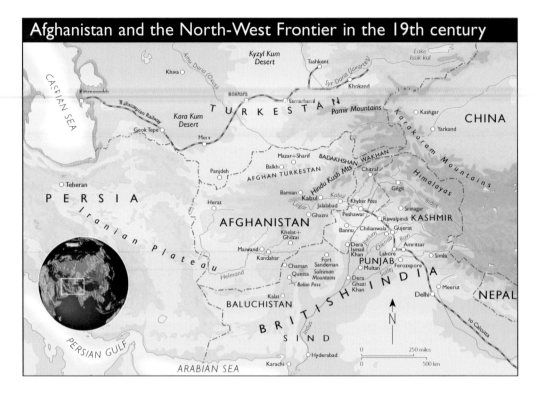

Russian forces to withdraw both from Turkey's European possessions as well as from the borders of Afghanistan. But British apprehensions were far from allayed. Even as the Congress was beginning its proceedings in Germany, a Russian diplomatic mission under General Nikolai Stolietov appeared, without invitation, in Kabul. Sher Ali, who had carefully avoided entanglement with either Britain or Russia, was placed in an invidious position, for he had just refused the dispatch of a British mission from India. The Amir stalled before being rescued from an unwanted agreement with Russia by Stolietov's recall by St Petersburg, a consequence of changing circumstances brought about in Berlin.

Nevertheless, Lytton was furious to discover the presence of a Russian envoy in Kabul. He repeated his demand, approved by Parliament on 14 August – even after Stolietov's departure – that the Afghan government must receive a British mission, whose purpose was to gain Sher Ali's agreement to the following terms, all of which stemmed from an erroneous belief

that Russia was seeking to manipulate Afghan foreign policy. Indeed, the last and most important point in what amounted to an ultimatum clearly, though not explicitly, referred to Russia:

1. The reception of British missions in Kabul whenever the Indian Government deemed it necessary.
2. The establishment of a permanent British military mission at Herat; and possibly Balkh and Kandahar as well.
3. The need to seek British approval before negotiating with any other country.

Refusing to ignore Sher Ali's failure to reply, Lytton warned him that a refusal to receive a British mission would be interpreted as an unfriendly act, one that might oblige British India to disavow its treaty obligations to Afghanistan. Accordingly, he dispatched Sir Neville Chamberlain who, on reaching Jamrud at the head of the Khyber Pass on 21 September with a British mission, was bluntly informed that his advance would be opposed by force. Chamberlain's mission, a mere escort and heavily outnumbered by the Afghan force sent to meet it, duly declined to proceed, signalling to the Viceroy that evening that the die had been cast: 'The first act has been played out; and I do not think that any impartial looker-on can consider any other course has been left open to us consistent with dignity than to openly break with the Amir.' Lytton concurred: any continuation on Sher Ali's part to refuse to accept a British mission, while welcoming into the capital a Russian envoy, he explained to the Secretary of State for India, 'has deprived the Amir of all claim upon our further forbearance' and must inevitably require a mission's installation in Kabul by British troops.

Notwithstanding Stolietov's withdrawal from Kabul – and thus the removal of any *casus belli* – and divisions of opinion within his government, the Disraeli administration permitted Lytton a strong degree of latitude in dealing with Sher Ali. Accordingly, on 2 November the Viceroy sent the Amir an ultimatum, demanding an apology and stating that he must agree by the 20th to receive a British diplomatic mission in Kabul, barring which troops would invade his domains. Such a prospect appeared entirely remote, for Sher Ali, as Chamberlain amusingly put it, 'had no more intention of apologizing than of turning Christian and applying for a Bishopric'. In desperation, Sher Ali sought military assistance from Kauffmann, but by the time he had heard back, the ultimatum had expired and Anglo-Indian troops were already across the frontier, leaving the Afghans with no prospect of military aid from General Kauffmann, who informed the Amir that none could be offered while the passes through the Hindu Kush were blocked with snow. The Amir panicked, fleeing north to open direct contact with the Russians and appointing his son, Yakub Khan, as regent, while at dawn on 21 November Anglo-Indian troops crossed the frontier.

NCOs of the 8th (The King's) Regiment of Foot during the Second Afghan War. (National Army Museum)

Warring sides

Following the Indian Mutiny (1857–58), the forces of the EIC were disbanded and their regiments absorbed into the regular British Army or the newly created Indian Army. The latter continued to maintain three armies based on the presidencies of Bengal, Bombay and Madras, but with critical lessons applied: improved pay and conditions in Native regiments and the deployment of a much larger number of regiments of the British Army to India to keep the proportion of British/Native forces closer to parity. Thus, whereas just prior to the Mutiny the ratio of British to indigenous troops stood at approximately 1:7, on the eve of the Second Afghan War the ratio had changed radically to 1:2, with 65,000 Queen's troops and 130,000 regular Native troops in India, all armed with the single-shot, breech-loading, bolt-action Martini-Henry or Snider rifles, weapons much more accurate than their smoothbore predecessors carried into Afghanistan a generation earlier.

As compared with the public's suspicious and critical attitude towards its soldiers at the beginning of Victoria's reign – by which time their high reputation attained under the Duke of Wellington in Spain and at Waterloo had largely faded – the British Army had by the time of the Second Afghan War acquired an exalted, heroic status. This shift was due to the fact that in the 40 years since the previous campaign in Afghanistan, the Army had established an unbroken record of achievement against the Sindis, Baluchis, Sikhs and Chinese in the 1840s, the Russians and Indian mutineers in the 1850s, the Burmese, Maoris, Abyssinians and the Chinese again in the 1860s, and the Ashantis in the early 1870s. All such feats were well known to large segments of an increasingly literate society, whose insatiable appetite for imperial adventure was fuelled

British infantry advancing swiftly during the Second Afghan War.

by new generations of war correspondents. The typical ranker, known sentimentally as 'Tommy Atkins', was portrayed as stalwart, indomitable and brave beyond his European counterparts, the noble defender of Empire and propagator of Western 'civilization'. If perhaps crude and unsophisticated, he stood above all 'savage' opponents, whose superiority lay only in their number, though at times even many Britons confessed to a grudging admiration for their courage. Many contemporaries extolled their own soldiers' virtues in song, poetry and hagiographic novels and newspaper reports. As one officer observed:

> From close contact with the British soldier, and a personal experience extending over many years, I can honestly say that some of the grandest qualities which go to make a noble character in man, I have seen over and over again exemplified in him, who [is] so unshaken in discipline, so patient in suffering, so ready for any sacrifice or service in the cause of Queen and country!

Major-General Sir Charles Napier pursuing tribal forces in Sind during his conquest of the region in 1843. (Author's collection)

In their first conflict with the British, the Afghans maintained no standing army, relying entirely on the spontaneous gathering of local militias and disparate groups of mountain tribesmen. By the time of the second war, Sher Ali had established a regular force estimated at 62 regiments of infantry totalling some 37,000 men, 16 regiments of cavalry and 49 batteries of artillery, principally deployed in and around the main cities of Kabul, Kandahar and Herat. The infantry employed an array of firearms, some as outdated as the old Brown Bess from the Napoleonic era, while others carried the latest Sniders and Enfields supplied, ironically, by Britain before the war. Artillery batteries contained six horse-drawn guns, while elephants, mules or bullocks hauled the mountain guns so essential for operations in a region with scarcely any roads designed for wheeled transport. The artillery, only a small proportion of whose guns were rifled and breech-loading, was nevertheless thought the best arm of the service, notwithstanding the varying age of the ordnance it brought into the field, and it performed well in the course of the conflict. While British and Indian forces on the subcontinent exceeded 200,000, only a small proportion of this impressive figure could be employed on foreign service; thus, the three columns formed for the invasion totalled only 29,000 men and 140 guns – and yet still constituted the largest force to serve outside India until 1914.

The fighting

Unlike the disastrous invasion of nearly 40 years before, the invasion of Afghanistan in November 1878 was to be conducted via three routes, and with a different objective in view: the pacification of the frontier areas and the destruction of the Amir's army, rather than his removal from power. The three routes of invasion were as follows.

In the north, a column of 10,000 men of the Peshawar Valley Field Force under Major-General Sir Samuel Browne, moving from Peshawar to Jalalabad via the Khyber Pass. In the centre, the Kurram Valley Field Force, a small column of 6,600 men and 18 guns under 46-year-old Major-General

Major-General Sir Frederick Roberts. One of the greatest Victorian commanders, he won the Victoria Cross during the Indian Mutiny before taking part in several minor campaigns in Africa. As commander-in-chief during the Second Afghan War, he achieved fame for a series of stunning victories and an epic march from Kabul to Kandahar. (Author's collection)

Frederick Roberts, to proceed from Kohat through the Kurram Valley, over the Peiwar Kotal to the Shutagardan Pass, and finally the 50 remaining miles to Kabul. Finally, in the south, the Kandahar Field Force of 12,800 troops and 78 guns under Major-General Sir Donald Stewart, to advance from Quetta to Kandahar. In total, the three columns numbered some 29,000 troops and 140 guns.

While Stewart reached Kandahar on 8 January 1879 after an unopposed march, the two other columns met opposition from both Afghan regulars and tribesmen, the latter of whom, consisting mainly of Afridis and Mohmands, plagued the lines of communication as the main forces extended into Afghanistan, obliging the British to deploy a reserve division to occupy their attention. Roberts, a Victoria Cross holder from the Mutiny described as 'a diminutive, red-faced, bandy-legged gamecock with the bearing of a lightning rod', found his progress held up by Afghan regulars. They were well ensconced in prepared positions, with artillery in support, on the summit of a ridge overlooking a narrow pass at the Peiwar Kotal, a hill 9,000ft above sea level covered in cedar pines. With the 5,000 Afghans under Karim Khan enjoying both numerical superiority and a commanding position above the valley in which Roberts was situated, a frontal attack was out of the question. After reconnoitring the area, he determined that a difficult though not impossible route up a valley to the right would place his troops on the Afghans' extreme left, theoretically enabling Roberts to attack the enemy in the flank. Accordingly, as a ruse he left a small force of two battalions of infantry and two squadrons of cavalry to his front and proceeded by night up the snow-covered track on 1 December, taking with him a force of 2,250 men, consisting of Highlanders, Gurkhas, two battalions of Punjab Infantry, a pioneer battalion, a mountain battery and four guns from the Royal Horse Artillery mounted on elephants. To protect themselves from the bitter cold, for the first time the soldiers wore puttees, or leg bandages, a feature of military dress thereafter so well associated with imperial troops. The Afghan defenders consisted of eight regiments of regular infantry and 18 guns mounted in carefully prepared entrenchments.

Amidst frosty conditions the column struggled up the steep hillside, making its way gingerly and surreptitiously around boulders and across streams, with baggage mules frequently losing their footing on the loose shale. Delay occurred when Roberts altered the order of march, but when dawn broke on the 2nd the Gurkhas and 72nd Highlanders stood at the base of the Spingwal Kotal, where the Afghans observed them. Immediately the Gurkhas began to ascend the mountainside, driving off their opponents westwards from their first *sangar* and, in conjunction with a company of Highlanders, carried on to seize a second entrenchment, followed around 7.30am by a vital third, which commanded the head of the pass. Having taken the Spingwal Kotal, Roberts then heliographed the camp 2,500ft below, ordering a frontal attack while he himself continued to force back the Afghan line, notwithstanding the difficult, precipitous, heavily forested and broken ground which not only hindered movement, but rendered command and control difficult to maintain.

By the early afternoon, Roberts' force was nearly upon the Afghan rear, while one British and one Punjabi battalion were advancing up the Peiwar Kotal from the valley, with guns of the Royal Horse Artillery shelling the Afghan camp, causing camels to stampede, tents to burst into flame and drivers and camp guards to panic and flee. With their line of retreat threatened, the Afghans abandoned 18 guns and dispersed, with Bengali cavalry in pursuit. Amongst the spoils of war, the victorious troops

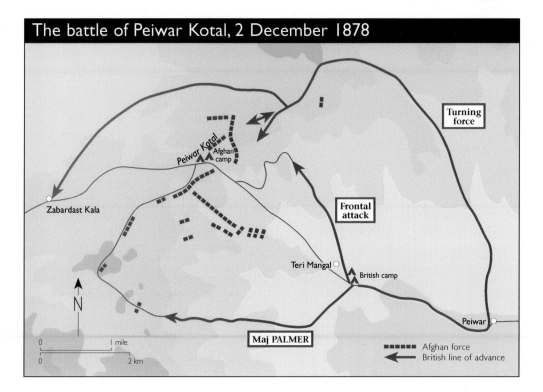

The battle of Peiwar Kotal, 2 December 1878

Peiwar Kotal

Afghan camp

Turning force

Zabardast Kala

Frontal attack

Teri Mangal

British camp

Peiwar

N

0   1 mile
0   2 km

Maj PALMER

▰▰▰▰▰ Afghan force
◀ British line of advance

British infantry and pioneers advancing against a stockade on the ridge north of the main Afghan position on the Peiwar Kotal, 2 December 1878. A country blessed with topographical advantages accruing heavily to its defence, Afghanistan consists of more than merely bleak and sun-baked valleys and precipices, as the wooded mountainside depicted here attests.

discovered a document, thought to be issued by Sher Ali, calling for *jihad*. 'Wage a holy war on behalf of God and his Prophet, with your property and your lives,' it ran. 'Let the rich equip the poor. Let all die for the holy cause. A foreign nation, without cause or the slightest provocation, has made up its mind to invade our country and conquer it ...' And thus far, the invasion was succeeding; Roberts' victory at Peiwar Kotal established what was to become a brilliant military career, for at great risk to his force he had managed to drive off a numerically superior opponent from a strongly defended position, at a cost to his own force of only 20 officers and men killed and 78 wounded.

Roberts continued to advance through enemy country, and by 9 December was reconnoitring a satisfactory route to the top of the Shutagardan Pass, with a dangerous

descent through its rugged features yet to come, but with the route to Kabul now open. With no means of defending his capital, Sher Ali issued an appeal for military assistance from the Russian diplomatic delegation, but Kauffmann refused to be drawn into hostilities and, in any event, observed that snow now blocked the passes through the Hindu Kush. The Amir, he therefore advised, ought to accept what terms he could secure. Not content with Kauffmann's refusal to help, Sher Ali left Kabul with the Russian mission on 13 December and proceeded to Russian-occupied Turkestan with the intention of continuing on to St Petersburg, still hopeful he could maintain his throne if the Tsar would plead his case before the Congress of Berlin. The Amir duly reached Tashkent, but no further, for he had yet to receive approval for the continuation of his journey into Russia proper.

Meanwhile, the second column, Browne's Peshawar Valley Field Force, entered the Khyber Pass and marched as far as the formidable fort of Ali Masjid, which the Afghans under Faiz Mohamed held with 3,000 regular infantry, 200 cavalry and

General Sir Samuel Browne, commanding the Peshawar Valley Field Force, enters Jalalabad, 20 September 1878. (Author's collection)

artillery mounted in smaller fortifications on both flanks. The whole force was situated on a hill 500ft above a gorge, and supported by 600 tribesmen in the hills on either side of the main position. Browne, expecting to be blocked at this juncture, had dispatched one brigade on a flanking march through the mountains north of the Khyber to re-emerge behind the Afghans, while a second brigade ascended the hills to confront the enemy's left and a third moved up for a frontal assault. This last brigade, consisting of the 81st, the 14th Sikhs and one Punjabi regiment, attacked on 21 November, but failed to penetrate the defences, obliging Browne to halt his offensive by sundown. The Afghans, meanwhile, on discovering the attempt to turn their position and fearing encirclement, quietly withdrew further up the pass, where they came into contact with British and Sikh troops who rounded up many of them as prisoners, making possible Browne's progress to Jalalabad.

All three columns were now deep inside Afghan territory, with the Kurram and Peshawar field forces regularly in contact with tribesmen contesting their presence. Still, the war appeared, even at this early stage, close to a conclusion, for on Sher Ali's withdrawal from Kabul to Turkestan, Yakub Khan, his son, had assumed power as regent, and shortly thereafter Sher Ali died. In February 1879, Yakub Khan, unwilling to carry on resistance and dismayed by British penetrations as far as Shutagardan and Gandamak with Kabul their ultimate objective, offered to discuss terms. Lytton maintained a low opinion of Yakub Khan, describing him as 'a very slippery customer whom we shall be well rid of if he disappears'. Many factors, however, suggested the wisdom of peace at this moment: the army was suffering badly from an outbreak of cholera; the campaign was proving extremely costly; Parliament was haunted by the possibility of a second disaster in Afghanistan; and Liberal opposition MPs under Gladstone were gaining increasing support against Disraeli. Lytton felt himself constrained to negotiate.

The fort at Ali Masjid during the Second Afghan War.

Major Sir Louis Cavagnari, Lytton's representative and Browne's political officer, sent a statement on 7 March detailing the essential preliminary basis upon which the negotiations must rest:

1. The renunciation by the Amir of authority over the Khyber and Michni Passes and the surrounding tribes.
2. Pishin, Sibi, and the Kurram Valley as far as the Shutagardan Pass to remain under British protection and control.
3. The regulation of the Afghan government's external relations in conformity with British advice and wishes.
4. Permission to station British officers, with suitable escorts, in Afghanistan.

On 26 May, Cavagnari and Yakub concluded a treaty at Gandamak, near the place where the 44th had made its last stand in 1842. British authorities in India agreed to recognize Yakub as Amir, who accepted the presence of accredited British diplomats in Kabul. The treaty ceded the Kurram Valley to British India and handed control of the Khyber Pass and of Afghan foreign policy to British authorities back in Calcutta. For his part, Yakub would receive an annual subsidy

of six *lakhs* of ruppees and the promise of Anglo-Indian protection from external aggression – a thinly veiled reference to Persia, but above all to Russia, the primary threat in the 'Great Game'. Two of the field forces, the Peshawar Valley and Kandahar, both wracked by cholera, would be withdrawn, the former immediately and the latter as soon as climatic conditions permitted. Roberts' column would, however, remain in the Kurram.

The circumstances confronting the invading forces strongly dictated the British decision for peace. The hardship suffered by Browne's troops, for instance, was acute, with temperatures in June above 110°F, and dust and thirst only adding to the trials of cholera. As the Official History recorded:

… especially as they made their final marches, their distress was very apparent. Their cloth[es] were stiff and dirty from the profuse perspiration and dust; their countenances betokened great nervous exhaustion, combined with a wild expression difficult to describe; the eyes injected, and even sunken, a burning skin, black with the effects of sun and dirt; dry tongue; a weak voice; and a thirst which no amount of fluids seemed to relieve. Many of these men staggered rather than marched into their tents and threw themselves down utterly incapable of further exertion until refreshed by sleep and food ... Nor did the officers appear to be in any better plight.

Cavagnari was fluent in Pashtun, well versed in the political affairs of the North-West Frontier and a competent officer. He now assumed the position of head of the diplomatic mission in Kabul. In July he left Roberts' headquarters, keen to take up his post and optimistic about the future – as opposed to Roberts, who had reservations about the longevity of peace given the restlessness of the country. Cavagnari proceeded with a small escort of 75 troopers and 50 *sepoys* of the Corps of Guides, an elite Indian mounted unit from the North-West Frontier. The Amir had promised him safe passage on the 60-mile journey to Kabul, where he arrived on 24 July and established his residence in the Bala Hissar. All appeared well in the city and Cavagnari was confident that his stay would be peaceful and that the countryside would remain quiet, sentiments he expressed in a telegraph message to the Viceroy's summer residence at Simla, in northern India:

Embassy [i.e. the diplomatic mission] entered the city and received most brilliant reception. Four miles from city sirdars with some cavalry and two elephants met us.

We proceeded on the elephants with a large escort of cavalry. Outside the city two batteries of artillery and nine regiments of infantry were drawn in column ... their bands playing the British National Anthem. Large crowd assembled and was orderly and respectful. Amir enquired after Viceroy's health and Queen and Royal Family. Amir's demeanour was most friendly.

But circumstances were not what they

Major Sir Louis Cavagnari, diplomatic representative of the Governor-General of India, Lord Lytton, negotiating with the Shinwaris for the safe conduct of Anglo-Indian troops on the road from Dakka to Lundi Khana during the Second Afghan War. He joined the ranks of other British diplomats who met a sticky end in Central Asia during the 19th century. (Author's collection)

The Afghan Amir, Yakub Khan (far left) and Major Cavagnari (to his right) sign the Treaty of Gandamak, 26 May 1879. By all appearances, this agreement ought to have concluded the Second Afghan War; but peace was fleeting. (Author's collection)

seemed, for there was deep resentment of Cavagnari's interference in native affairs and the liberality with which he distributed funds left tribal leaders with the impression that he, and not Yakub Khan, steered the tiller of state. Yakub, bitterly resentful, provoked trouble. When in August Afghan troops returning from Herat took up residence in cantonments at Sherpur, having themselves not participated in the recent campaign and therefore not tarred with the brush of defeat, they openly demonstrated their resentment at Cavagnari's presence and voiced disgruntlement at the government's failure to pay them in a timely fashion. Arriving at the Bala Hissar early on the morning of 3 September to collect their wages – three months in arrears – they received less than expected and anger turned to fury. When a rumour spread that money was to be had at the British Residency

nearby, the crowd of troops arrived en masse, startling the escort who fired a shot, upon which the Afghans withdrew to collect their weapons and ammunition.

The Anglo-Indian position at the compound now stood in peril. The Residency itself consisted of a handful of small, flat-roofed buildings surrounded on several sides by other structures and lacking an adequate perimeter wall. The troops made the best they could of a poor situation by fortifying the grounds, while Cavagnari sent word to Yakub Khan, requesting assistance. The Amir sent his young son and a *mullah*, together with an escort of Afghan cavalry, but the gathering mob merely jeered and pelted them with stones. Matters turned uglier when the mob joined the 2,000 Afghan troops on their return, upon which the assault commenced.

The opposing sides consisted of four British and 75 Indian soldiers on the one hand, and thousands of Afghans on the other. Cavagnari was killed at an early stage in the fighting, followed by two other officers, but Lieutenant Walter Hamilton and his Guides continued resistance from atop the roofs and by sallying forth on sorties, bayonets at the ready, against the crews of artillery deployed against the Residency. In due course the Afghans set the buildings alight, the number of defenders dwindled and Hamilton died leading another sortie. By nightfall only a handful of *sepoys* were left standing, all of whom repeatedly and scornfully rejected calls for surrender and quarter, appeals having been made to them by their co-religionists. Twelve hours into the fight, the survivors made a final sortie from which none returned, adding the defence of the Residency, in which perhaps 600 attackers fell, to the many other heroic actions of which the Victorian era is replete.

No sooner had news of the action reached India (on 5 September) than orders for the withdrawal from Kandahar were countermanded. Roberts set off from the Shutagardan Pass en route to Kabul with a new column rapidly gathered at Kurram and known as the Kabul Field Force, consisting of two infantry brigades of seven battalions in total, one brigade of cavalry composed of four regiments, and four batteries of artillery – in all 6,500 men ready to march by 27 September with the aim of avenging

Cavagnari's death. Meanwhile, Yakub Khan, in a bid to mollify both sides and remain in power, called for resistance from his own people – specifically the frontier Ghilzais – while simultaneously appealing to the British for help. But Roberts was not conciliatory, sending envoys back with a stern reply: '… so long as the bodies of those officers and men remain unburied or uncared for in Kabul, I do not believe the English people will ever be satisfied. They will require the advance of a British force, and the adequate punishment of the crime …' Yet no sooner had Roberts set off for the Shutagardan Pass on 30 September than Yakub Khan arrived at his camp, expressing regret for Cavagnari's death, claiming his helplessness at preventing the uprising and applying for protection from his own mutinous troops whom he claimed had deposed him. Above all, he wished for Roberts to halt his advance. To Roberts' mind, the Amir's words constituted nothing more than a ruse to ascertain the strength and intentions of Anglo-Indian forces and pass this information on to his own via the

Sikh troops in action against Zaimmukht tribesmen at Zawa, in the Kurram Valley, December 1879. (Author's collection)

Theatre of operations during the Second Afghan War, 1878–81

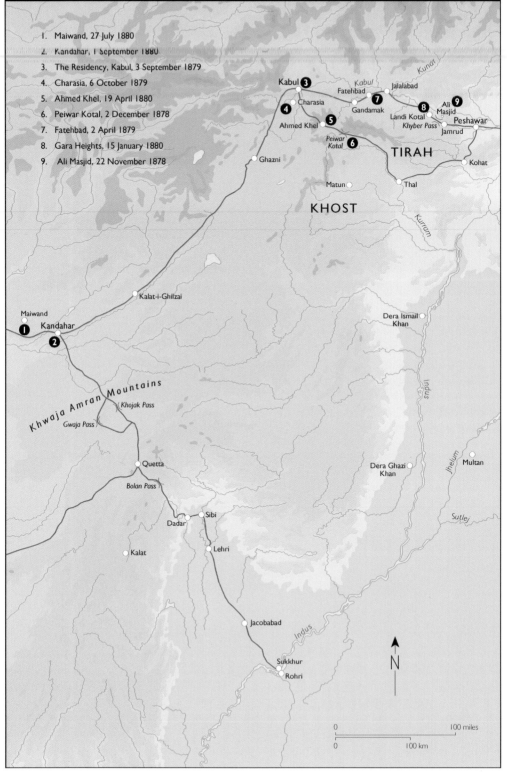

1. Maiwand, 27 July 1880
2. Kandahar, 1 September 1880
3. The Residency, Kabul, 3 September 1879
4. Charasia, 6 October 1879
5. Ahmed Khel, 19 April 1880
6. Peiwar Kotal, 2 December 1878
7. Fatehbad, 2 April 1879
8. Gara Heights, 15 January 1880
9. Ali Masjid, 22 November 1878

escort. Without any conclusive proof, however, Roberts was obliged to allow Yakub to remain, and the column duly set off, though the shortage of transport prevented Roberts from moving more than one brigade at a time.

In the event, Roberts' suspicions proved well founded, for intelligence soon reached him that at least 13 regiments of Afghan regulars were concentrating along a range of hills at Charasia, 12 miles south of Kabul. Outnumbered by four times his own number, Roberts appreciated that he must confront this force as quickly as possible, before reinforcements arrived. When on 5 October he arrived at Charasia, standing before a series of hills pierced by a single defile, Roberts possessed only his leading brigade, with the next in support still a day's march away. With inadequate numbers of troops to take and occupy the hills before sunset, he decided to force his way through the defile on the following day, thus adopting the plan he had employed with such success at Peiwar Kotal. When the sun rose, however, he found progress impossible, for the regular Afghan troops occupied positions above him, while tribesmen were assembling to attack his camp. Worse still, an Afghan force of unknown size had manoeuvred between himself and the next brigade behind, under Brigadier-General Herbert Macpherson. With only 4,000 men and 18 guns, and with Afghan strength continually rising, Roberts had to make a decision: immediate assault.

At dawn, Roberts had sent forward a force to reconnoitre the defile, but the Afghans had responded by positioning a large force on either side of it. Roberts consequently chose to pin the enemy in that position, sending the brigade under Thomas Baker in an outflanking manoeuvre westwards to attack the more vulnerable extreme Afghan right. With Highlanders at the forefront, the brigade advanced up the precipitous heights in the teeth of serious opposition from both Afghan regulars and tribesmen. Major Reginald Mitford recorded his impressions of the 92nd on this occasion:

> The dark green kilts went up the steep rocky hillside at a fine rate though one would occasionally drop and roll several feet down the slope, showing that the rattling fire kept up by the enemy was not all show. Both sides took advantage of every available atom of cover, but still the kilts pressed on and up, and it was altogether as pretty a piece of Light Infantry drill as could well be seen.

Major-General Sir Frederick Roberts and his staff inspecting captured artillery at Sherpur, outside Kabul, in October 1879.

The Highlanders were soon joined by Gurkhas and Punjabi infantry, the combined force dislodging the defenders as they progressed towards the summit overlooking the defile. The Afghans, perceiving this, moved troops to their right, only to find themselves weakening another sector and permitting British and Indian infantry to reach the heights and make contact with the men of Baker's brigade. With two regiments of Highlanders and a mix of Gurkhas and Indians pressing inexorably forward by early afternoon, the Afghans, leaving 12 guns and several hundred dead on the field, gave way and fled, pursued by light cavalry.

With the Afghans routed, Roberts entered Kabul, a city of 50,000 residents, without resistance on 13 October. Yakub Khan abdicated, although Lytton could think of no suitable successor. Until one could be found, Roberts was ordered to remain in the country in what the Afghans interpreted as an indefinite sojourn, notwithstanding a British pledge to leave once an acceptable ruler could be found, based on consultations with the principal chiefs. In the meantime,

Roberts set about rounding up those responsible for the September uprising and the deaths of Cavagnari, his fellow officers and the Guides, a stern warning of which had come two days after Roberts' arrival with the following proclamation:

> The force under my command has now reached Kabul and occupied the Bala Hissar; but its advance has been pertinaciously opposed, and the inhabitants of the city have taken a conspicuous part in the opposition offered. They have, therefore, become rebels against the Amir, and have added to the guilt already incurred by them in abetting the murder of the British Envoy and his companions.

The alleged culprits were hanged in front of what remained of the Residency and, sharing the fate of the Great Bazaar in 1842, the Bala

Execution of the Kotwal of Kabul on 26 October 1879 in front of the remains of the British Residency where Cavagnari, his staff and escort had been killed the previous month. (Author's collection)

Hissar was destroyed as a warning against further violence. With winter approaching, the troops gathered supplies, fortified the Sherpur cantonment a mile north-east of the city and built accommodation. The perimeter measured 4½ miles in length, with a ridge to the north and loop-holed walls around the other three sides, rendering the south and west easily defensible but the east wall incomplete. The addition of *abattis* and wire entanglements and the placement of 20 pieces of artillery completed Roberts' preparations for winter quarters, but with only 7,000 troops, composed of 5,500 infantry (three British, one Gurkha and five Indian battalions), it was far from adequate.

And so it proved. In December, hoping to recover from their humiliating reverses and retake Kabul, Afghans began to gather from provinces across the country, encouraged by their religious leaders' call for a *jihad* against the invaders. They concentrated around Kabul, thousands of whose inhabitants left the city to join their armed compatriots poised to attack Roberts' position. Yet rather than await the inevitable assault by overwhelming numbers, Roberts took the initiative and chose to confront the separate elements of his adversaries' forces before they could combine and destroy him through sheer weight of numbers.

Despite a positive start, his plan was marred by the failure to ambush the Afghans to the west of the city, when Brigadier-General Dunham Massy failed to adhere to his orders. Massy nearly lost his entire force of 300 troopers and four pieces of horse artillery to the 10,000 Afghans under Mohamed Jan, into whom he blundered on 11 December, but in his hasty retreat the four guns were abandoned. For the next three days, severe fighting took place, the Afghans driven from the heights to the south and south-west of the city. Still, with his opponents' numbers rapidly rising, Roberts realized that he had no choice but to withdraw into the relative safety of Sherpur. The Afghans reacted immediately, swarming down only to meet determined resistance

from the Anglo-Indian and Gurkha defenders, who by the 14th were safely ensconced in Sherpur as the Afghans reoccupied Kabul.

Here Roberts sat in isolation, his telegraph lines severed, the heliograph useless owing to cloudy conditions, and while reinforcements were on the way from Gandamak, overwhelming enemy numbers suggested the brigade would not reach the besieged cantonment. Meanwhile, amongst the Afghan populace, the fanatical *mullahs* were encouraging the flames of revolt, planning a general assault on Sherpur for the 23rd of the month. Roberts had intelligence warning him of the attack; his troops stood at the ready, lining the walls of the cantonment through the night until, as a flare exploded in the darkness signalling the offensive, great hordes moved rapidly across the snow against the east and south walls, bearing scaling ladders and urged on by *ghazis*.

The Special Correspondent of the *Daily News*, assigned to cover the campaign, reported how in the distance 'came a roar of voices so loud and menacing that it seemed as if an army 50,000 strong were charging down upon our thin line of men'. At the opposite end of the cantonment, British troops found themselves involved in fierce fighting. 'Suddenly … arose a din as if every fiend in hell had broken loose,' remembered Mitford.

> The undercurrent or base was one ceaseless roll of musketry broken at frequent intervals by the roar of a heavy gun. Above this rose British cheers and Sikh war-cries answering the yells of the Moollahs and Ghazis, screams, shrieks, and noises of every hideous description. Add to this that the bullets were whistling about us, knocking up the stones, splintering the abattis, and tearing through the empty tents, and you may form a very inadequate idea of the scene on which the peaceful stars looked down.

The British regulars held the south wall, while Punjabis and Guides held the east, discharging a series of fusillades with artillery in support. Despite serious casualties suffered in the face of disciplined fire, the Afghans continued with their determined onslaught until approximately ten in the morning when, after an hour's respite, they resumed their assault, though with somewhat diminished ardour. By 1.00pm on Christmas Eve, the Afghans had given up the effort and were withdrawing rapidly, leaving hundreds of their number strewn around the cantonment. Then, the gates swung open and lancers, Guides and Punjabi light cavalry thundered after the fleeing Afghans, whose numbers were reckoned to have been 100,000, against which the Anglo-Indians had lost only three dead and 30 wounded. The following day all was quiet, the enemy having withdrawn not only from the city, but the hills and villages, as well.

With the start of 1880, the countryside appeared peaceful, but there was as yet no provision for replacing Yakub Khan. Yet colonial officials back in India were not going to repeat the mistake of 1842 and order the troops' precipitous withdrawal from Afghanistan without establishing some reliable form of government; until such time, Lytton wrote in October 1879, the army would remain:

I think we should instantly take possession of the authority which falls from the hand of the Amir into our own and promptly, though provisionally, enforce that authority, so far as our practical power of enforcing extends, in every direction … The next step will be either to proclaim our permanent retention of that authority or to transfer it, with very careful and copious restrictions, to some form of native government.

Success over opposing forces spelled the end of a British scheme originally proposed to divide Afghanistan into separate provinces, a course of action predicated on the notion that it would be easier to control the country's unruly tribes and would avoid the necessity for an army of occupation. There

remained the issue of a suitable Amir now that Yakub Khan had abdicated and was receiving a pension in India. Abdur Rahman, a nephew of Sher Ali, did not initially meet an acceptable standard, as for the previous dozen years he had been receiving a pension from the Russians as a result of his efforts in 1863 to secure the Amirship for his father – the Russians' preference – instead of Sher Ali. Yet despite his apparent unacceptability, Abdur Rahman was considered the best available candidate by Lytton, who was anxious to withdraw British troops from Afghanistan as quickly as possible lest the Russians be provoked into an intervention of their own, or the country dissolve into a state of anarchy. In any event there was growing opposition to the war at home from the Liberals under Gladstone. Finally, as the grandson of Dost Mohamed – considered by many to be the greatest recent leader of Afghanistan – Abdul Rahman was less likely to appear to his people as a mere puppet, installed by a foreign power, and enjoying no popular support. The British also soon found a governor for Kandahar, which Sir

Reinforcements under Brigadier-General Gough, bound for Kabul, find their path blocked by Afghan forces at the Jagdalak Pass, January 1880. (Author's collection)

The battle of Maiwand, 27 July 1880

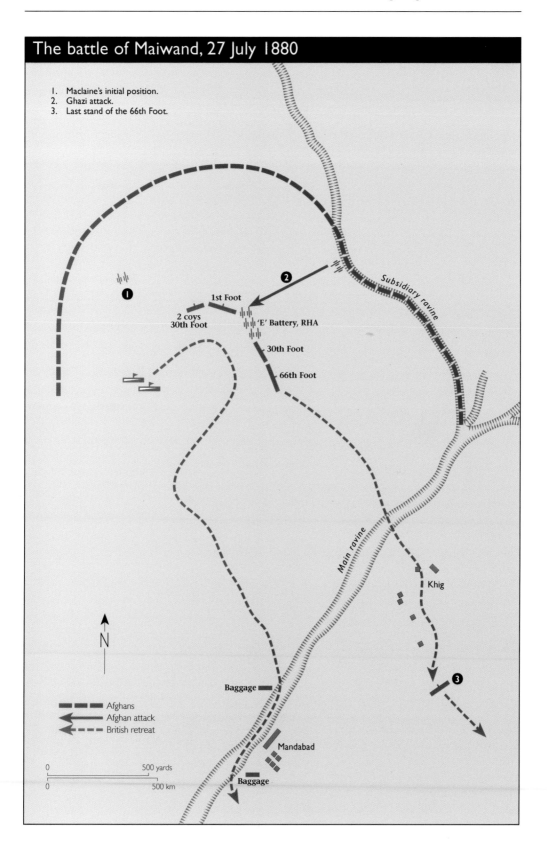

1. Maclaine's initial position.
2. Ghazi attack.
3. Last stand of the 66th Foot.

①

②

1st Foot

2 coys
30th Foot

'E' Battery, RHA

30th Foot

66th Foot

Subsidiary ravine

Main ravine

Khig

③

Baggage

Mandabad

Baggage

N

— — — Afghans
←——— Afghan attack
←- - - - British retreat

0   500 yards
0   500 km

Donald Stewart re-occupied before devolving command to General James Primrose, an officer in the Bombay Army.

Stewart proceeded north where he encountered considerable resistance at Ahmed Khel, about 20 miles west of Ghazni, by a strong force of Ghilzais and other tribes, as on previous occasions driven to a pitch of fanaticism by accompanying *mullahs*. On 19 April, 3,000 sword-bearing tribesmen launched a furious attack on the Anglo-Indian centre at Ahmad Khel, with cavalry swarming on the flanks in a bid to reach the rear of Stewart's line, formed in haste. 'Down they came,' Lieutenant-Colonel E. F. Chapman recalled, 'quite regardless of our fire ... the whole hill seemed to be moving.' The 59th Foot was nearly overwhelmed, but managed to hold on until a battalion of Gurkhas and another of Sikhs, with strong artillery in support and aided by a Punjabi cavalry charge, steadied the line. After bringing in his reserves, Stewart held on, the savage fight continuing for a further two hours before the Afghans retired. Stewart entered Ghazni without firing a shot on the 21st, and two days later left 400 dead and wounded tribesmen on the field at Arzu, seven miles to the south-east, at a cost to himself of only two dead and eight wounded – the stark result when sword-armed assailants met well-trained, disciplined, rifled-armed regulars in open country.

On reaching Kabul in late April, Stewart learned that he was to succeed Roberts and that the government in London had fallen, with a Liberal ministry under Gladstone in office. Lytton, whose support for Abdur Rahman had waned, had resigned, to be replaced as viceroy by Lord Ripon, who like Stewart could summon up but little enthusiasm for the candidacy of Abdur Rahman. Nevertheless, as support was rising within Afghanistan itself, British authorities gradually decided that he should rule the country and duly proclaimed him Amir on 22 July. Hardly had a week passed, and as troops were on the verge of leaving Kabul for the return march to India, than news arrived of the annihilation of Primrose's Bombay division and the siege of Kandahar, 320 miles south-west of Kabul, by 7,500 well-equipped Durani tribesmen under the fiercely anti-British prince, Ayub Khan. He planned, after the fall of the city, to eject the remaining British troops from the country by means of a popular revolt and assume the throne himself.

The troops in question were those of Brigadier-General George Burrows, who on

Indian cavalry charging at the battle of Maiwand, 27 July 1880. Like all Victorian campaigns apart from the Crimea, British troops relied heavily on indigenous and other non-European contingents to support them in Afghanistan, especially Indians from Bengal and other regions, Sikhs from the Punjab and Gurkhas from Nepal. (National Army Museum)

14 July was dispatched from Kandahar to support the Wali of Kandahar in the area around the Helmand River in the south of the country. By that time, Ayub's army, which had been able to assemble without interference in distant Herat, had made substantial progress towards the Helmand before Burrows had even got underway. Burrows' force consisted of an infantry brigade containing one Queen's regiment (the 66th), the 1st and 30th Bombay Infantry, one battery (six guns) of Royal Horse Artillery, a company of sappers and two Bombay cavalry regiments. When the British arrived at the Helmand, in sight of the Wali's encampment, the Afghans simply decamped, abandoning Burrows with a scratch force of only 2,700 men, 80 miles from the nearest support, while Ayub was growing hourly in strength through tribesmen flocking to his cause, together with elements of the Wali's deserters. Burrows, aware that he had to defend the approaches to Kandahar, however inadequate his force, withdrew to Khusk-i-Nakhud, 35 miles back, where he was instructed to prevent Ayub from circumventing Kandahar in an effort to take Ghazni while en route for Kabul.

Despite efforts through reconnaissance to ascertain the location of Ayub's main body, Burrows remained ignorant of his enemy's dispositions, apart from receiving intelligence on 26 July that local tribesmen held the village of Maiwand, 13 miles to the north-east of his present position. Intending to take the village and block Ayub's presumed line of advance, Burrows discovered on his approach the following day that Ayub had already arrived with the whole of his force, consisting of between 15,000 and 20,000 regulars and tribesmen, supported by 30 guns. Burrows failed to make best use of available ground, deploying his forces in line in an exposed position instead of making use of nearby buildings and a *nullah* (small ravine). Matters were desperate from the outset, for the Afghans had the advantage in both numbers and guns, rendering Burrows' position completely hopeless. His men held their

Fighting back-to-back, soldiers of the 66th Foot make their last stand at Maiwand, 27 July 1880. (Author's collection)

ground for a while, but his cavalry refused to charge. When one of his inexperienced *sepoy* regiments began to falter under the pressure, another gave way altogether, causing a panic that left the Indian troops mingling amidst the 66th, which with its ranks disturbed could no longer offer regular fire against their attackers. The single available British battery fought as long as it could until it was obliged to limber up to avoid capture, and the 66th managed to withdraw gradually towards the buildings for what little cover they offered. There, together with a handful of Indian soldiers, the regiment fought until annihilated. Burrows' losses numbered 1,100 dead, with a few survivors reaching Kandahar after a dreadful retreat. As indicated earlier, Ayub followed up his victory by laying siege to the citadel of Kandahar, garrisoned by the remainder of Primrose's force, 5,000 men and 13 guns – almost certainly enough, with the adequate stocks of food and ammunition at their disposal, to withstand a storm. Still, as an added precaution against the possibility of an Afghan rising in the city, Primrose expelled the entire population of 15,000 inhabitants.

How the war ended

To Roberts – who, owing to his popularity, retained senior command of Anglo-Indian forces in Afghanistan – restoring British prestige in India and relieving the beleaguered garrison in Kandahar required a swift and decisive blow against Ayub Khan. Thus, on 11 August, after feverish preparations, Roberts' field force of 9,900 men and 18 guns left Kabul and made for Kandahar – a forbidding, almost impossible march of more than 300 miles. His force consisted of 12 battalions of infantry: the 60th Rifles, the 72nd and 92nd Highlanders, plus Sikh, Gurkha and Punjab infantry, a cavalry brigade, including the 9th Lancers, mules carrying light mountain batteries and as little baggage as possible to ease the speed of movement. Roberts' march would enter the annals of British military history as one of the Army's greatest feats. Struggling across mountains and deserts under a blistering sun during

the day and temperatures plunging to freezing at night, Roberts' forces carried on undaunted at an average rate of 15 miles a day, without so much as a line of communication back to Kabul. And yet, on 31 August, after a forced march of 313 miles in 21 days over extremely difficult terrain – albeit with no fighting en route but with serious losses from sickness – he reached Kandahar and joined the garrison there. Ayub had raised the siege and taken a strong position near Dubba, two miles to the north-west of the city. Notwithstanding the exhaustion of his troops and his own ill-health, Roberts launched an attack on the following day, spearheaded by a bayonet assault by the 92nd Highlanders and 2nd Gurkhas. This inflicted 1,200 casualties and drove Ayub's forces off in confusion at a cost to Roberts of only 40 dead and 228 wounded – extraordinarily low in return for such a decisive outcome.

The 92nd (Gordon) Highlanders skirmishing with Afghan tribesmen during the Second Afghan War. (Author's collection)

Indian *dollie* carriers bearing wounded troops through the Jagdalak Pass, January 1880. (Author's collection)

The defeat of Ayub Khan spelled the end of the British proposal for the break-up of Afghanistan and its partial occupation by Anglo-Indian forces. In the course of great debate about the possible permanent garrisoning of Kandahar, this scheme was rejected, and all British and Indian troops evacuated the country. Abdur Rahman was left to rule over his turbulent domains and the treaty concluded with him entitled British India to the districts of Pishin Sibi near Quetta, the Kurram Valley and a protectorship over the Khyber Pass, home of the turbulent Afridis. No further trouble resulted between Afghanistan and British India during Abdur Rahman's period of rule. The Russians did not – just as they had not after the First Afghan War – interfere in

As a consequence of a rising of the Afridis on the North-West Frontier in 1897 which resulted in the fall of the Khyber Pass, British authorities in India dispatched General Sir William Lockhart with an expedition to the Tirah Valley, where 2,000 of his men clashed with two-and-half times their number on 20 October at the Dargai Heights, the key action of the largest frontier expedition ever mounted by British forces, involving a total of 35,000 men. While forming up the Gordon Highlanders for attack, Lieutenant-Colonel Mathias declared: 'Highlanders! The general says the position must be taken at all costs. The Gordons will take it!' (Author's collection)

Afghan internal affairs, and the British administration in India was left to manage as best it could the unruly tribes of the North-West Frontier, which while a constant running sore proved a fertile training ground for British troops well into the 20th century.

Arthur Male, Army chaplain, 13th Hussars

Amongst the many memoirs and first-hand accounts on the Second Afghan War, that of an obscure Army chaplain named Arthur Male provides particularly fine insights into the campaign. Attached to Sir Samuel Browne's headquarters, he witnessed various operations from the unusual perspective of a junior officer with an ostensibly non-combatant role (except *in extremis*), and he remained throughout the war in close contact with the higher echelons of field command.

His explanation for his presence with the Army reveals much about his opinion of the simple Victorian soldier, making sacrifices in a land remote from home and for a cause of which he was most probably ignorant:

And how comes it that I, a minister of religion, should be thrown into association with scenes of blood and carnage …? Simply because the English nation, when it sends its gallant soldiers into the field, credits them with something more than mere physical frames to be kept strong and in good fighting trim. 'Tommy Atkins,' while he has a strong arm to strike for his country, has a heart also to feel and sympathise. He is a *man*, not a machine; and has needs other than those which can be met by the daily meat ration, the third of an ounce of tea, or even the rum ration.

The column under Sir Samuel Browne approaches the seemingly impregnable fortress at Ali Masjid, in the Khyber Pass, 22 November 1878. (Author's collection)

It will be recalled that when in late 1878, the Amir failed to answer Lord Lytton's ultimatum demanding the admission of a British diplomatic mission to Afghanistan, three columns of British, Indian and Gurkha troops crossed the frontier, one originating from Peshawar and led by Major-General Browne. Browne was a veteran of the Sikh Wars and holder of the Victoria Cross, the Army's greatest decoration. He earned the medal, like Roberts, during his service in the Mutiny, where leading a mounted irregular unit he killed in single combat a rebel carrying a standard, in the course of which he lost his left arm – and hence his innovation, still in use today, of the Sam Browne belt. He held the admiration and loyalty of Indian and Queen's regiments alike, and troops were prepared to follow him to the ends of the Earth. Browne's first objective, it will be recalled, was the mighty fortress of Ali Masjid in the strategically important rocky gorge well known in the annals of the British Army: the Khyber Pass.

It was in this peculiar capacity that, amongst many other reminiscences of his time in Afghanistan, Male recorded the

The fortress of Ali Masjid, which the Peshawar Valley Field Force, consisting of three brigades under Sir Sam Browne, discovered occupied by an enemy force during his advance on Jalalabad in November 1878. While a frontal assault failed to dislodge the garrison, Browne's turning movement persuaded the Afghans to abandon the position without further resistance.

attack on Ali Masjid. When his column, composed of three brigades of troops, approached the fortress, Browne ordered Tytler to march his brigade over the hills around the enemy's right in a wide arc, bringing his forces to the rear of the fort. By this disposition, Tytler would cut off the Afghan retreat in the event either that the main attack should succeed in expelling them or that the garrison should choose to abandon the place as untenable. Tytler was to march as soon as darkness descended, so enabling him to reach his position by dawn. Meanwhile, Macpherson, with his brigade, was to begin his march four hours before dawn and occupy the Shagai Heights, on the enemy left, thus clearing the hills on Browne's right while Appleyard's brigade marched along the valley to strike the main Afghan position.

The orders were rapidly conveyed. Tytler's brigade, consisting of the 1/17th, a regiment which had served in the First Afghan War, the 1st Regiment of Sikhs and the Guides, began its movement as the sun set over the horizon. Macpherson's brigade, of Rifles and Gurkhas, marched several hours later, well under the cover of darkness. The following morning, 21 November, just after dawn, Browne's column led by Appleyard's brigade with its six regiments – four Indian and two British, together with a mountain battery and another of 40-pdrs drawn by elephants – entered the Khyber and proceeded towards Ali Masjid, as Male recorded in his memoirs:

Afghan tribesmen, perched behind the cover of a *sangar*, or rock-lined redoubt, fire down on enemy troops. (Author's collection)

The golden glory of the Eastern dawn flooded even the gloomy recesses of the Pass, as the men, European and native, pressed on, braced up somewhat by the keen air of the early morning. Presently, emerging from the narrower defile, the scenery changed. On both sides there rose a succession of undulating hills, until away in the distance, a mile and a half or so, one could see Fort Ali Musjid strongly placed on a rocky plateau, some 600 feet above the bed of the river, which flowed in breaks and shallows along the valley below. Impregnable indeed it seemed, by its very position, frowning down from beetling crags … It was built of hard mud, faced with stone, with numerous guns. The slopes, both above and lower down, bristled too with *sungahs* [*sangars*], a special form of Afghan defence consisting of strong walls of stone, behind which dense bodies of men took up position. Now and again guns were mounted here too.

Browne halted his men for a period to allow the elephant battery to reach its position up the narrow paths that composed the crude and treacherous route. After a brief rest, the bugles sounded the attack, echoing along the mountains as the 81st Foot and 14th Sikhs pushed forward a line of skirmishers to clear the enemy from the hillsides on their flanks, while at the same time a battery of artillery galloped up into position and began shelling the guns of the fort. But the Afghans intended to stand their ground, and immediately returned effective fire, as Male recorded:

And now the crash of the shells as they exploded, and the constant rattle and roll of the rifle fire made valley and mountain side alive with deafening reverberation. The men pressed on with impetuous valour; but the wild defenders of fort and *sungah* were nothing daunted. Gun answered gun, while crowds of Afghan warriors could be seen rushing out to man the outer entrenchments, and even streaming over the hillside.

With the arrival of the elephant battery came the hoarse boom of the 40-pdrs, striking at the mud and stone walls of the fort, gradually silencing the Afghan guns and creating gaping holes in the walls with explosive shells. Still, as Male appreciated, the most difficult task was yet ahead, for the *sangars* had to be taken and the fortress itself stormed if this vital route to Kabul was to be secured. The slopes were littered with these defences, all containing concealed parties of riflemen and one or two pieces of artillery. Male watched as a Captain Maclean, leading a party of Sikhs rushing one such entrenchment, fell wounded to enemy fire, together with seven NCOs and 20 rank-and-file as casualties. Lying at the foot of a *sangar*, Maclean called for support, which arrived in the form of Major Henry Birch at the head of the 27th Punjabis, who advanced against heavy small arms and artillery fire.

Male watched as the hail of rifle fire now met this new target with devastating effect:

> Down went Birch, shot dead, his face towards the foe, and round him thickly fell his men. They wavered; then fell back, with the remnant of Sikhs, and the wounded Maclean. Birch's subaltern, young Fitzgerald, would not brook that his chief's body should lie there exposed to the wanton ferocity of the fanatics, who were used to mutilate with such unnameable barbarity. He called for volunteers from his own Punjabis to bring in the body of their leader. But alas! the Afghan fire still fiercely swept the slope, and there was no response. Turning to the Sikhs, who were forming up again near by, their one officer lying desperately wounded, he shouted for some of them to follow him; and fifteen gallant fellows rushed forward to climb again the slope of death. Up they went, step by step, one and another falling here and there. Halfway up Fitzgerald was struck, but with heroic resolution he still pressed on, intent on his task of rescue. He reached the body of Birch, raised it in his arms, when a bullet again struck him, and he fell dead; the two friends thus side by side in the sleep of death, almost within touch of the Afghan guns.

Almost none of the 15 men involved in the assault returned alive – the consequence of a failure to lay down adequate preparatory fire to support the infantry. With the strength of the enemy's defences better appreciated, a battery of horse artillery came forward, clattering over stone and river bed before unlimbering and shelling the *sangars*. Yet the Afghans' fire proved overwhelming, driving off the Punjabis and Sikhs, decapitating a gunner, wounding several more and injuring a number of horses. Additional guns now arrived in the form of a heavy field battery and a mountain battery, deployed to support elements of the 51st Foot which, guided by their cool-headed colonel, crossed a stream, which Male watched with great suspense:

> On they went, and began to climb the slippery hillside in support of the native troops. For a moment the Afghan fire seemed checked. But ere this final, and, perhaps, decisive movement could be developed and carried out the shadows of the night descended, as they do in Eastern lands, all too suddenly, and the bugles were heard sounding the 'Retire'. Even as the men, Punjabis and Sikhs, fell back unwillingly, the Afghans, recovering, swept again the slope with parting volleys, and many another was added to the list of killed or wounded.

The assault having failed, and with no further prospect of success that day, Arthur Male, in his capacity as chaplain, now reflected on the sullen aftermath of battle and undertook one of the principal, yet mournful, duties of that role – responsibility for conducting burial services for the fallen:

> The after-scenes of a battle-field are never pleasant. When actual fighting has ceased, and fierce passions are somewhat allayed, men have time to pause and to think, and then the saddest thoughts gather in upon one. On this occasion, however, there was scarce time for mental rest, or pause or thought. The fierce struggle was to be renewed at dawn; for the position must be ours at all costs.

For the living there was a meal and much-needed sleep; but for the dead their remains had to be interred. The crew of a battery composed the body of one of their own, finding a few coins in his pocket and a letter from the man's sister, written amid the pleasant surrounding of the country home, now sharing with the stricken soldier the carnage scenes of the battle ground, and almost, too, the alien grave. And thus one and another were consigned to the quiet resting-place of mother earth's bosom. And the living looked round for some soft spot where they might take a lighter sleep.

In fact, there was to be no further fighting the following day, and no opportunity to redeem their losses with a successful storm, for Tytler's wide flank march had succeeded in occupying the village of Kata Kushta, behind the Afghan position, effectively cutting off the enemy's line of retreat. On learning of this, the Afghan commander panicked, abandoned his guns, tents, food and other supplies, and made a bid to withdraw under cover of darkness, only to blunder straight into positions occupied by the 17th Foot, the 1st Sikhs, and the Guides, who having remained on the alert through the night, simply rounded up large numbers of enemy troops, caught utterly unawares and unable to mount a defence. And so it was that Male, accompanying Browne and his staff, struggled up the steep slopes and entered the crumbling fort, on whose ramparts a soldier quickly ran up the Union Jack.

Opposite page:
An air raid being conducted by a Handley Page V/1500 on an Afghan position, May 1919.

PART III
The Third Anglo-Afghan War, 1919

Origins and background of the war

In the wake of the Second Afghan War, Anglo-Indian forces conducted dozens of minor operations along the North-West Frontier, most notably in the Tirah Valley, around Malakand, and elsewhere, but relations with Afghanistan, though strained at times, remained civil, if not altogether friendly. During World War I (1914–18), British and Indian forces were necessarily diverted to the Western Front, Gallipoli, Palestine and Mesopotamia (modern Iraq). Very fortunately for administrators in India, however, Anglo-Afghan relations stood on a friendly, even cooperative, basis.

Such was largely owing to the policy of neutrality helpfully pursued throughout the conflict by the Amir, Habibulla, to whom the Sultan of Turkey, an ally of Germany, had appealed as leader of the Muslim world to join the *jihad* against the Allies. Though anxious to prevent a joint Turkish–German mission from appearing in Kabul during the war, lest he risk criticism from his domestic pro-Turkish opponents, Habibulla prevaricated and blocked requests for action against Britain. He went so far as to bar tribal leaders from operating against British possessions along the frontier, even while *mullahs*, hoping to bring Afghanistan into the war on the side of the Central Powers, sought to raise the banner of revolt amongst the tribes.

Any such revolt would have come at a critical time, for much of the Indian Army was operating overseas and British reverses in Gallipoli and the Middle East emboldened those preaching resistance to the authority of Anglo-Indian rule. Much of the credit for the security of the frontier also lay with the Chief Commissioner of the North-West Frontier Province, Sir George Roos-Keppel, who earnestly cared for the welfare of the Pathans who inhabited parts of this region, was fluent in their language and enjoyed their full confidence and trust. Thus was it possible, during World War I, for him to maintain order over most of the frontier, though two tribes, the Mohmands and the Mahsuds, did rebel in 1915; the former were subdued by a blockade, while the latter were not quelled until two years later owing to the dearth of disposable troops along the Frontier.

Thus it was that as Ross-Keppel prepared to step down from his post in January 1919, he confidently informed Lord Chelmsford, the Viceroy, that the frontier was peaceful with a favourable prospect of a quiet summer. Yet his prediction was flawed, for with the renewal of peace in Europe and the Middle East, Habibulla hoped to receive from Britain some compensation for the policy of cooperation he had adopted during the conflict, not least owing to the great danger in which he had placed himself from those still angered by his failure to assist Turkey. Specifically, he sought to reassert his country's right to manage its own foreign affairs and thus rescind one of the principal terms of the treaty that had concluded the Second Afghan War. The viceroy was, however, prepared to consider Afghan requests and thus Anglo-Afghan differences did not appear irreconcilable.

Yet before talks could begin, the Amir was assassinated in his tent with a rifle shot, to be succeeded by his brother, 27-year-old Nasrulla, in contention for the title of Amir with Habibula's third son, Amanulla. As governor of Kabul, Amanulla had access to the treasury and arsenal of Kabul and, with the support of the army, he arrested Nasrulla, charged him with Habibula's murder and sentenced him to life imprisonment before proclaiming himself Amir on 28 February. Amanulla shared his father's desire to free Afghanistan of foreign control, a position shared by general opinion across the country.

In ousting from power his uncle and other conservative elements in society, however, the new Amir placed himself in a precarious position. By April 1919, it was clear that he had to find some method of placating both the conservative and progressive elements of society in order to remain in power. Moreover, as the army suspected him of complicity in his father's murder, Amanulla felt obliged to placate the troops with increased pay, and even seriously contemplated a campaign to recover Peshawar as a distraction to his domestic woes.

While nationalism continued on the rise in Afghanistan, so too were rumblings of dissent in India, where a nascent independence movement had sprouted before World War I. Riots broke out in the Punjab with fatal consequences, when on 11 April troops under Brigadier-General Rex Dyer fired on a crowd in Amritsar, resulting in the deaths of 379 people and injuries to another 1,200. No further disorder arose, but the tragedy had a profound effect on Indian public opinion and encouraged Amanulla, whose advisers misled him as to the true extent of Indian dissent, to condemn the British for what he described as heavy handedness against a people who had loyally supported them in the war. More critically, he expressed support for the justice of Indian nationalist aspirations and, to prevent any unrest spilling across the border, announced his intention to move troops up to the Durand Line, the line of demarcation established between British India and Afghanistan in 1893. 'Gird up your loins,' he told the tribal chiefs two days after Amritsar, 'the time has come.' Another *jihad* was under way.

It is not clear if Amanulla intended to invade India or simply sought to benefit from any disorder that arose in the Punjab, whether by the deployment of his own troops or through the instigation of a revolt of the tribes. Whichever option he chose, or if he merely threatened either course, this patently anti-British stance would distract attention from his domestic problems, not least the religious divisions within Afghanistan, and consolidate support from otherwise disputatious factions. Whatever the Amir's intentions, his commander-in-chief, Saleh Muhamed, drew up a plan for an incursion into India. British authorities had arrested at Peshawar an Afghan postmaster, whose papers revealed the outbreak to commence on 8 May, to coincide with the appearance of Afghan troops in the North-West Province. The uprising never came to pass, not only owing to the authorities warning Roos-Keppel beforehand, but by a premature Afghan crossing of the border by 150 Afghan troops at the western end of the Khyber Pass five days before the planned rising. This incursion resulted in the occupation of the village of Bagh, the source of the water supply for the 500 *sepoys* of the Khyber Rifles stationed on the nearby Landi Kotal. Much of the Afghan countryside had already responded to the Amir's call, and thousands of tribesmen converged on Jalalabad, stimulating the Indian government to order general mobilization.

While the full extent of Afghan intentions was not known, Roos-Keppel nevertheless advised Chelmsford to eject the Afghan troops from Bagh before local tribes rose in their support. The garrison at Landi Kotal had not been fired upon, but it could not defend itself without urgent reinforcement. At the same time, the main seat of authority in the province, at Peshawar, where mobs of Afridis rioted in the bazaars, had to be secured to avert any possible insurrection. A mere battalion was available to assist the Indians at Landi Kotal, and on 7 May this was rapidly transported by a convoy of several dozen heavy lorries through the Khyber. On the same day, British authorities closed off Peshawar with a cordon of troops and police, and threatened to deny water to the city unless the ringleaders were handed over. This demand was duly met and the following day Peshawar was out of danger and business resumed in the bazaars. Further British and Indian reinforcements were now moved up the Khyber, bringing the strength of troops at Landi Kotal to a brigade, under Crocker, and on 9 May it attacked the Afghan positions at Bagh.

Warring sides

The Afghans at this time maintained a regular standing force of approximately 50,000 men, organized into 75 battalions of infantry, 21 cavalry regiments and 280 modern pieces of artillery. To supplement these forces, the government in Kabul could call upon as many as 80,000 tribesmen operating in an irregular capacity. To oppose them, the Indian Army maintained eight divisions, five independent brigades and three brigades of cavalry, not including Frontier Militias. Formidable though they were in numbers, their quality could no longer match those of the 1914 Indian Army, for many of its best troops had been lost in the fighting in France and the Middle East, and with many regiments still overseas awaiting demobilization, those left behind in India were composed of green recruits.

With respect to units of the British Army, of the 61 regiments stationed in the subcontinent in 1914, all but eight infantry and two cavalry regiments had been sent overseas to fight. Their places were filled by territorial units composed of part-time soldiers originally intended for the defence of the United Kingdom, but who had, when mobilized at the outbreak of the war, volunteered for overseas service and been sent to India to replace regular units who were deployed to the Western Front or, later, the Middle East. Morale was low: after four years of dull service in India the soldiers were anxious to return home and were not keen to fight the Afghans – so much so that many were inclined to disobey any call for active deployment and only declined to carry out their intentions upon the direct appeal of the commander-in-chief in India. If both Crown and Indian Army forces suffered from deficiencies in manpower and morale, compensation could nevertheless be found in technology, with machine guns, armoured cars, radio communications, motorized transport and aircraft all used in the war.

Afghan officers during the third Anglo-Afghan War, 1919. (Photo by Hulton Archive/Getty Images)

The fighting

When on 9 May Anglo-Indian troops attacked the Afghan positions at Bagh, half the attacking force had been detached to protect the northern flank, leaving insufficient numbers with which to capture all their objectives. Still, some success was achieved when three Royal Air Force (RAF) aircraft launched a raid on tribesmen at Dacca, just over the border in Afghanistan. Two days later the British resumed their attack, this time with 18 pieces of artillery and 22 machine guns covering the lead attack executed by the 2nd North Staffordshires and two battalions of the 11th Gurkhas, who forced the Afghans back at the point of the bayonet. RAF planes strafed the Afghans as they retired back over the frontier. Ross-Keppel, seeking to ensure that the Afghans did not renew their offensive into India, determined upon a pursuit as far as Dacca, where the British camp found itself bombarded from artillery at long range as well as the object of an infantry attack. Aircraft were to play a central part in his strategy, as he explained to Chelmsford's private secretary:

> There will shortly be a big collection of troops and tribesmen at Dakka. We can use aeroplanes to smash up their encampment at Dakka. We have twenty-four aeroplanes here, and an attack on Dakka and possibly on Jalalabad from the air would not only take the heart out of the Afghans but would give all those who are at present half-hearted a very good excuse for pulling out.

Capture of the fortress at Spin Baldak by Anglo-Indian troops during the Third Afghan War, 27 May 1919. A late 19th century structure situated on the road from the Bolan Pass to Kandahar, it could not withstand modern artillery and aerial bombardment. In the foreground Sikh crews man a mountain battery, but in reality the artillery deployed was field pieces of the Royal Artillery. The fort fell after hand-to-hand fighting between British infantry (background) and Afghan regulars.

The British repulsed the assault and launched a counter-attack the following day, but it was not until 17 May that the Afghans withdrew from their positions, leaving their guns behind. Operations nevertheless continued to be hindered by unanticipated unrest developing in the rear of the British position extending through the Khyber Pass, held by the Khyber Rifles. This indigenous force, which had served loyally in actions as recently as 1908, began losing men via desertion, and with discipline failing and disaffection growing, Roos-Keppel felt compelled to disarm and disband the corps. Moreover, with additional trouble brewing in and around Peshawar, troops were dispatched to observe the situation and quell any potential revolt. As a means of striking at the heart of the disaffecting influence, Chelmsford chose to attack Afghanistan itself, and ordered his force to continue the advance from Dacca to Jalalabad.

No sooner was this offensive meant to get underway than circumstances in the south took a turn for the worse. Together with the attack through the Khyber Pass, the Afghans had planned two others: one in the Kurram, and the other against Quetta. The British reacted from Quetta first, though, crossing the frontier and capturing the fortress of Spin Baldak on 27 May, forestalling any further Afghan activity in the south, but not affecting affairs further north where circumstances appeared less heartening. In Khost, west of the Kurram Valley, General Nadir Khan, the best of the Afghan leaders, led 14 battalions totalling 3,000 well-equipped troops, but his intentions were unknown to his British counterpart, Brigadier-General Alexander Eustace. Believing that Thal, at the southern end of the Kurram Valley, appeared the likeliest target, he sent reinforcements, bringing local strength up to only 800 young and inexperienced Indian troops, with four mountain guns and two mortars. There also remained the possibility that the Afghans would attack further south, in the upper Tochi Valley, defended by the North Waziristan Militia who could not be expected to hold their position without assistance from regular forces, of which Eustace could provide none. He therefore ordered the militia posts to be evacuated, upon which the Wazirs of Tochi rebelled and the Waziris and Afridis within the militia deserted or were otherwise deemed unfit for purpose.

Mutiny arose throughout the area, particularly around Wana, the base of the South Waziristan Militia, where *sepoys* raided the treasury and a store of ammunition. Only through the most trying circumstances was the commandant, Major Guy Russell, able to survive his break-out to safety by moving south with a small contingent of loyal militiamen, suffering under a terrible sun and constant attack by tribesmen and rebel *sepoys* until his force made contact with a relief force of militia from Zhob. Disaffection had proved the undoing of several units, including the South Waziristan Militia, which was disbanded, together with much of its northern counterpart. The Khyber Rifles also ceased to exist on the basis that, with authority broken down throughout Waziristan, British authorities could no longer rely on such units, dependent upon recruitment of local levies, for frontier security.

How the war ended

Notwithstanding the lawlessness gripping Waziristan, British authorities had higher priorities than restoring order there. Nadir Khan had moved against Thal, laying siege to the town on 27 May. There, Eustace suffered from a number of disadvantages: fewer troops and guns than his adversary, a shortage of supplies and an inexperienced Indian force, none of whom had served in the Great War. All told, it was not clear if he could defend the place for an extended period and a new division, moving from Lahore to Peshawar and intended for an advance on Jalalabad, was directed instead to Kurram, where elements were detached to garrison the undefended town of Kohat. At the same time, a brigade under Dyer was directed to move hastily to relieve Thal. But Dyer was the wrong man for the job. Plagued by illness and suffering from fatigue, his reputation has been tarnished by the Amritsar massacre. Moreover, his troops, were of uncertain quality: made up of Territorials keen to demobilize and local troops of indifferent quality, although he did have some reliable Gurkhas and Punjabis. However, Dyer showed himself capable of inspiring them, and though short of food and water and seldom taking rest on the march under a blazing sun from Peshawar, his forces covered ground rapidly until they found both the northern and southern routes to Thal blocked. Dyer's biographer recorded the situation thus:

> At Togh, the General addressed his troops, exhorting them to make a great effort to rescue their comrades at Thal. His words touched the hearts of that strangely assorted force of veterans and war levies, Punjabi peasants and London men of business so that they marched to the last of their strength; some of them dropped in their tracks. At four o'clock in the morning on 31 May they set out along a fairly open valley between steep hills. There was no wind and but little water, and as the day advanced the stony hillsides became a furnace, the naked rocks throwing back the sun so that it seemed to strike from the ground as from the sky.

Deploying his guns against both enemy bodies, Dyer began firing as he ordered forward his infantry against the Afghans' southern position. The artillery sufficed to force the tribesmen to withdraw before an infantry battle ensued, and by the end of the day Thal lay open to Dyer's forces.

On the following day, 2 June, Dyer launched an offensive to the west; but at this point Nadir Khan sent forward an envoy bearing a flag of truce and requesting a ceasefire. As his troops were already fully committed to the fight, Dyer resumed the attack, but before making contact the Afghans withdrew westwards, with armoured cars, aircraft and cavalry in pursuit. Both sides concluded an armistice on 3 June. Militarily, Dyer had finished the war on a successful note, but the Amritsar incident continued to plague him. Notwithstanding his insistence that he had prevented a general insurrection in the Punjab, he was relieved of command and died a few years later in Britain.

The peace conference opened at Rawalpindi in July. The Afghans were in no mood to be conciliated, despite the fact that they had been evicted from Indian soil. After heated discussions a treaty was hammered out and signed on 8 August, with the Afghans achieving their principal aim: the right to conduct their own foreign affairs. Both sides reaffirmed the Durand Line as the border, and the Afghans made an important pledge not to interfere in the political affairs of the tribes along the North-West Frontier.

Conclusion and consequences

The First Afghan War, 1839–42

Notwithstanding the reoccupation of Kabul by Pollock's force in 1842, the reputation of British arms had suffered considerably as a consequence of Elphinstone's ill-fated retreat to Jalalabad, revealing that the forces of the British Army and EIC – albeit small in that particular campaign – could be overcome. Within the Company's forces themselves, particularly those of the Bengal contingent, some of the *sepoy* regiments had performed indifferently, and the bonds of trust between British officers and the *sepoys* had palpably weakened. In political perspective, Au Russian forces pport of their d British s; a ry Shuja's y at the ussian At great ar had gender Afghan heecifically British India. everse of Auckland's policy.

Virtually nothing had been achieved, for even a cursory examination of the outcome of the war reveals that the circumstances had hardly changed, except for the worse, since Auckland had launched his enterprise in 1839. The Russians continued to make territorial gains in Central Asia, and the EIC's armies had together lost 15,000 officers and men (mostly from disease), quite apart from many thousands of camp followers. Fifty thousand camels had died in the war and the cost to the Treasury amounted to nearly £20 million. Russia helpfully gave up its claim to Khiva and provided a number of other assurances to Britain about its intentions, but nothing had been achieved that could not have been accomplished through diplomacy.

The true extent of the whole disastrous enterprise came to light only a year after Elphinstone's sacrifice of the Army of the Indus, when Dost Mohamed returned to this throne, complete with British approval. There he would remain in power for two decades, not only peacefully inclined towards British India, but also unwilling to bow to the pressure of Russian expansionism. Most astonishing of all, when the Raj faced its greatest crisis of all and depended on non-interference from Afghanistan – during the great mutiny that was to engulf northern and central India between 1857 and 1858 – Dost Mohamed remained obligingly neutral. His neutrality freed British authorities to divert troops from the Punjab which, having only been annexed in 1849 after two conflicts with Britain, could well have staged a rebellion, and allowed them concentrate on the crisis around Delhi and in Oudh, hundreds of miles to the east.

The fundamental problem of the British plan in the First Afghan War lay around the fact that the principal aim, the replacement of a supposedly anti-British Amir with one favourably inclined towards London and Calcutta – what may now be termed 'regime change' – proved entirely unnecessary. Two central issues had not been properly examined when Auckland dispatched the expedition: firstly, the reaction that could be expected from the various Afghan tribes, all fiercely independent, to forcibly imposing on them a former ruler of Afghanistan with an uncertain degree of popularity; and secondly, an examination of the prospects of Anglo-Indian forces retaining control of the country, presuming that they could conquer it in the first place, itself a very speculative proposition. These were questions that exercised contemporaries but not, apparently, the Governor-General, at least not with sufficient depth. With remarkable foresight, Mountstuart Elphinstone, the former governor of Bombay who had been proposed as Governor-General in 1835 but declined it, outlined to a friend these very points on the eve of the invasion:

> ... we have [now] assumed the protection of the state [of Afghanistan] as much as if it were one of the subsidiary allies in India. If you send 27,000 men up the Bolan Pass to Candahar (as we hear is intended), and can feed them, I have no doubt you will take Candahar and Caubul and set up [Shah] Soojah; but for maintaining him in a poor, cold, strong and remote country, among a turbulent people like the Afghans, I own it seems to me to be hopeless.

In the event, of course, Anglo-Indian forces did take Kabul and establish Shah Shuja on the throne, but even William Elphinstone,

a month before his withdrawal from the capital, confessed to Macnaghten that the whole enterprise had been a failure:

> And yet, under the most favourable events, I would have you share the feeling which is growing strongly upon me – that the maintenance of the position which we attempted to establish in Afghanistan is no longer to be looked to, and that after our experience of the last two weeks [under siege and constant attack] it must appear to be, if not in vain, yet upon every consideration of prudence far too hazardous and costly in money and in life for us to continue to wrestle against the universal opinion, national and religious, which has been so suddenly and so strongly brought into array against us.

The Indian government made a pathetic attempt to claim victory in the form of a

The battle of Miani, the principal engagement of Sir Charles Napier's conquest of Sind in 1843, when he defeated the Baluchis and annexed their country, with its capital at Hyderabad. (Author's collection)

proclamation issued by Lord Ellenborough at Simla on 1 October 1843, exactly four years after Auckland had issued his own proclamation justifying intervention in Afghan affairs. Ellenborough went so far as to repudiate Auckland's policy while still shamelessly asserting that some good had emerged from the conflict:

Disasters unparalleled in their extent, unless by the errors in which they originated, and by the treachery in which they were completed, have in one short campaign been avenged upon every scene of past misfortunes; and repeated victories in the field, and the capture of the cities and citadels of Ghazni and Cabul, have again attracted the opinion of invincibility to the British arms.

The British army in possession of Afghanistan will now be withdrawn to the Sutlej. The Governor-General will leave it to the Afghans themselves to create a government amidst the anarchy which is the consequence of their crimes …

Content with the limits nature appears to have assigned to its empire, the government of India will devote all its efforts to the establishment and maintenance of general peace, to the protection of the sovereigns and chiefs, its allies, and to the prosperity and happiness of its own faithful subjects …

The enormous expenditure required for the support of a large force in a false military position, at a distance from its frontier and its resources, will no longer arrest every measure for the improvement of the country and of the people.

In summary, the war cost vast sums of money, though this was scarcely apparent in Britain, for the economic burden had fallen almost exclusively on the shoulders of the Indian revenue, crippling its finances for years to come. British intervention in Afghanistan had left no change except a legacy of mistrust and hatred by Afghans for

Britain. Dost Mohamed was Amir once again; Shah Shuja was dead, with his sons in exile in India, and the British were back on the Sutlej. Total and ignominious failure did not, on the other hand, appear to discomfort British authorities in the least, leaving some shockingly similar mistakes to be repeated less than four decades later: first, in the fact that the Russian threat had receded even before the war had begun; and second, that while prior to hostilities the Afghans were at least neutral and at best friendly, at their conclusion they stood justifiably hostile and resentful.

But perhaps the greatest damage done to Britain as a result of the war was psychological rather than political or financial, and thus som_____sis. The blow made a_____ not be entirel_____ victories ach_____ and inevit_____ the Comp_____ the day, _____ power in_____ sought to_____ for their ov_____ morale and _____ leadership, b_____ entirely efface_____ from Kabul. Only a han_____ probably those who deserted ranks in the first day or two – made it back to India as survivors of that harrowing episode, but they brought with them accounts of execrable British planning, shockingly incompetent leadership and instances of cowardice that must have eroded trust and weakened the bonds that existed between the Indian rank-and-file and their British officers. The Mutiny was still 15 years in the future, but there is some basis for the theory that the first seeds of the revolt were sown during the fateful year of 1842. Henry Lawrence, Chief Commissioner of the Punjab, numbered amongst many who supported this hypothesis:

At Cabul we lost an army, and we lost some character with the surrounding states. But I hold that by far our worst loss was in the confidence of our Native soldiery. Better had it been for our fame if our harassed troops had rushed on the enemy and perished to a man, than that surviving Sepoys should be able to tell the tales they can of what they saw at Cabul.

European soldiers and officers are placed as examples to Native troops, and a glorious one they have generally set in the field; but who can estimate the evil when the example is bad – when it is not the Hindustani (most exposed to cold, and least able to bear it) who clamours for retreat and capitulation, but the cry is raised by the men he has been accustomed to look up to and to lean upon as a sure resource in every emergent peril.

The Second Afghan War, 1878–81

While British policy had originally entailed dividing Afghanistan after the defeat of Ayub Khan, this was not pursued, notwithstanding some debate about the viability of occupying Kandahar for an extended period. In fact, as noted earlier, all British garrisons withdrew from the country and Abdur Rahman was left to consolidate his rule across Afghanistan, though with some territorial concessions granted to British India, including the strategically important areas of Pishin and Sibi, near Quetta, and the Kurram Valley, together with the power to oversee the Afridi country around the Khyber Pass. Relations with Abdur Rahman proceeded on a largely amicable basis in the years that followed the Second Afghan War, with Russia excluded from any involvement in the foreign affairs of the country, though she continued to expand beyond the Hindu Kush.

As with the first conflict, Indian government officials consistently believed the Afghans well disposed to at least limited British influence in Afghan affairs and, more remarkably, to leaders imposed from the

outside. In June 1879, in the wake of the Treaty of Gandamak, when peace seemed to have been secured for the long-term, Lytton explained to Cranbrook precisely these hopelessly optimistic and naïve terms:

I think you need be under no anxiety about the satisfactory execution and results of the Kabul Treaty or any troubles in Afghanistan consequent on the withdrawal of our troops ... The Afghans will like and respect us all the more for the thrashing we have given Sher Ali and the lesson we have taught to Russia ... The Afghan people certainly do not view us with any ill-will.

Such views, like those expressed during the first war, smacked of a dangerous misunderstanding of the Afghan mentality. Although from a military point of view the second war clearly ended on a higher note than the first, parallels nevertheless remain, not least in the manner in which the war resulted in a severe drain on the Indian treasury, quite apart from the human losses – approximately 8,000 deaths from disease and some 1,850 killed in action or died of wounds, while Afghan losses defy estimation. As in the first war, territorial concessions followed, with the strategically important Kurram Valley and Khyber Pass given over to British responsibility by Abdur Rahman. The ostensible cause of the second war, moreover – to limit Russian influence in Afghanistan – again in its basic terms resembled the motives behind the first and, as before, had never manifested itself as a bona fide threat.

If, as in 1842, Afghan relations with Britain had been soured, they were no better with the Russians, for whom Abdur Rahman entertained strong suspicions, especially as a result of the Russian incursions along the northern Afghan border that culminated in the annexation of Merv in 1884 and the occupation of the Panjdeh Oasis a year later. These events pushed Britain and Russia close to war and emphasized both to the Afghans and the British the need to clarify the precise

The citadel at Kandahar, showing the main gate, August 1880. (Author's collection)

demarcation of the hitherto vaguely defined North-West Frontier. In 1893, therefore, Abdur Rahman opened discussions with the government in Calcutta respecting a conference for this purpose. Sir Mortimer Durand and his mission duly arrived in Kabul on 2 October. After several weeks of discussions, the mission agreed on 13 November to raise the subsidy to the Amir in return for a treaty delineating the boundary from Chitral to Peshawar and from there to the point of juncture between Persia, Afghanistan and Baluchistan. The new border, stretching more than a thousand miles, became known as the Durand Line, and though it solved the problem between British India and Afghanistan, it never satisfied the various affected tribes who clung fiercely to their traditional independence and regularly defied Anglo-Indian attempts to put down their revolts, the first being in Chitral in early 1895. Thus, after Britain's second nearly fruitless conflict with Afghanistan, India was left with marginally greater security on its western fringes, but with the relentless task of policing that perennially troubled region, the North-West Frontier.

The Third Afghan War, 1919

The conclusion of the Third Afghan War did not end troubles for British authorities in India, for the fighting had caused unrest that could not be immediately quelled, especially in Waziristan, where the trouble deepened. The disbandment or break-up of militia units in the North-West Frontier was naturally seen by local tribesmen as an opportunity to foment trouble. The Mahsuds and Wazirs, though traditional rivals, found a common purpose in exploiting British weakness and uniting against them, making use of weapons and ammunition looted or brought to the field by deserters from the militia, who possessed a degree of military experience and training useful to the rebels. Thus began years of opposition to British authority, opposition that was to continue well into the 1930s.

The war was hardly over when, in November 1919, the British made their first attempt to subdue the insurrection, with Major-General Andrew Skeen operating against the Tochi Wazirs, with reasonable success. But the Mahsuds proved altogether more formidable opponents when, in early December, Skeen's largely green troops led by inexperienced officers failed to make inroads, and it was not until the action fought at Ahnai Tangi the following year that the Mahsuds suffered grievous losses – 4,000 casualties and the burning of their villages. Such injuries persuaded them, for the moment at least, to cease hostilities. There followed a British offensive in November 1920 against the Wazirs in the area around Wana, where opposition ceased the following month and the city was retaken. Minor operations continued as ethnic Afghan raids and harassing attacks continued during 1921, when the British responded with a new policy: the establishment of a permanent garrison of Indian Army regulars in Waziristan, in conjunction with reconstituted local militias (their predecessors having been disbanded during the Third Afghan War because of desertions), who would depend on the support of the former.

* * *

Taken together, if a lesson emerges from the experiences of the three Anglo-Afghan Wars it is this: that while modern, well-equipped armies can defeat their conventional Afghan counterparts, vanquishing their irregular compatriots in the countryside presents altogether more complex and perhaps insoluble military problems. The experiences of all would-be conquerors since ancient times seem to confirm this point, including the abortive Soviet attempt at occupation from 1979 to 1989 and NATO intervention since 2001. The mere establishment of a government at the behest of a foreign power is no substitute for one that enjoys broad support across the country, untainted by accusations that it serves a foreign master. The ethnic and linguistic diversity of the country strongly militates against all but strictly partisan allegiances to any but a domestically created populist government

capable of fostering – insofar as is possible in a land of such ethnic diversity and geographical remoteness – a national identity.

The problems faced by foreign powers bent on direct intervention in Afghanistan formed the basis of a letter written in 1842 by an extraordinarily prescient but sadly anonymous British officer, the accuracy of whose words of admonition apply as aptly today as they did in the early years of Victoria's reign:

> To conquer a dominion by controlling the political parties of a state is a feasible policy, or to reform by gradual means without annihilating the institutions of a subjugated country may be the effect of time and perseverance, but to subdue and crush the masses of a nation by military force, when all are unanimous in the determination to be free, is to attempt the imprisonment of a whole people: all such projects must be temporary and transient, and terminate in a catastrophe that force has ever to dread from the vigorous, ardent, concentrated vengeance of a nation outraged, oppressed and insulted, and desperate with the blind fury of a determined and unanimous will.

Since time immemorial, operations in Afghanistan have posed immense challenges to any power seeking to impose its will over this seemingly unconquerable region of Central Asia, where though technology has changed out of all recognition from the Victorian era, the nature of the fighting and the resoluteness of the enemy remains largely unchanged today. The challenge facing NATO forces today, therefore, must rest with their ability to apply successful principles of asymmetric warfare in the field, in combination with a fundamental reconstruction of the country's social, economic and political infrastructure – all challenges of considerably greater magnitude than those faced by Britain in the past.

Bibliography and further reading

General

David, Saul, *Victoria's Wars* (Penguin, 2007)

Dodwell, H. H., ed., *The Cambridge History of India*, (Cambridge University Press, 1932)

Duncan, John & John Walton, *Heroes for Victoria* (Spellmount, 1991)

Farwell, Byron, *Queen Victoria's Little Wars* (London, Harper & Row, 1972)

Ferguson, Niall, *Empire: How Britain Made the Modern World* (Penguin, 2004)

Fortescue, J. W., *A History of the British Army* (Naval & Military Press, 2004)

Hernon, Ian, *The Savage Empire: Forgotten Wars of the Nineteenth Century* (Sutton, 2000)

James, Lawrence, *The Rise and Fall of the British Empire* (Abacus, 2000)

Morris, James, *Heaven's Command: An Imperial Progress* (Penguin, 1979)

Armies, Weapons and Uniforms

Blackmore, Howard L. *British Military Firearms, 1650–1850* (Greenhill Books, 1994)

Barthorp, Michael, *The British Army on Campaign (1): 1816–1853* (Osprey Publishing, 1987)

Barthorp, Michael, *The British Army on Campaign (3): 1856–1881* (Osprey Publishing, 1988)

Beckett, Ian, *The Victorians at War* (Hambledon and London, 2003)

Farwell, Byron, *Mr. Kipling's Army: All the Queen's Men* (W. W. Norton & Company, 1981)

Featherstone, Donald, *Khaki & Red: Soldiers of the Queen in India and Africa* (Arms & Armour Press, 1995)

Featherstone, Donald, *Victoria's Enemies: An A-Z of British Colonial Warfare* (Blandford Press, 1989)

Featherstone, Donald, *Weapons and Equipment of the Victorian Soldier* (Blandford Press, 1978)

Harding, D. F. *Small Arms of the East India Company, 1660–1856*, 4 vols. (Foresight Books, 1997–99)

Haythornthwaite, Philip, *The Colonial Wars Sourcebook* (London, Arms & Armour Press, 1995)

Heathcote, T. A., *The Indian Army: The Garrison of British Imperial India, 1822–1922* (David & Charles, 1974)

Holmes, Richard, *Redcoat: The British Soldier in the Age of Horse and Musket* (HarperCollins, 2005)

Holmes, Richard, *Sahib: The British Soldier in India* (HarperCollins, 2001)

Knight, Ian, *Go to Your God Like a Soldier: The British Soldier Fighting for Empire, 1837–1902* (Greenhill Books, 1996)

Mason, Philip, *A Matter of Honour: The Indian Army, its Officers and Men* (Jonathan Cape, 1974)

Stewart, Jules, *The Khyber Rifles: From the British Raj to Al Qaeda* (Sutton, 2006)

Strachan, Hew, *From Waterloo to Balaklava: Tactics, Technology and the British Army, 1815–1854* (Cambridge University Press, 1985)

Strachan, Hew, *Wellington's Legacy: The Reform of the British Army, 1830–1854* (Manchester University Press, 1985)

Afghan Wars (general)
North-West Frontier/Afghanistan

Allen, Charles, *Soldier Sahibs: The Men Who Made the North-West Frontier* (Abacus, 2001)

Barthorp, Michael, *Afghan Wars and the North-West Frontier, 1839–1947* (Weidenfeld & Nicolson, 2002)

Docherty, Paddy, *The Khyber Pass: A History of Empire and Invasion* (Faber & Faber, 2007)

Edwardes, Michael, *Playing the Great Game* (Hamish Hamilton, 1975)

Elliot, Maj.-Gen. J. G., *The Frontier, 1839–1947* (Cassell, 1968)

Heathcote, Tony, *The Afghan Wars, 1839–1919* (Spellmount, 2003)

Hopkirk, Peter, *The Great Game: On Secret Service in High Asia* (John Murray, 2006)

MacMunn, Lt.-Gen. Sir George, *The Romance of the Indian Frontier* (Jonathan Cape, 1974)

Miller, Charles, *Khyber: The Story of the North West Frontier* (Macdonald and Jane's, 1977)

O'Ballance, Edgar, *The Afghan Wars, 1839 to Present* (Brassey's, 2002)

Richards, D. S., *The Savage Frontier: A History of the Anglo-Afghan Wars* (Pan, 2002)

Schofield, Victoria, *Every Rock, Every Hill: The Plain Tale of the North-West Frontier and Afghanistan* (Buchan, Enright, 1984)

Stewart, Jules, *The Savage Border: The Story of the North-West Frontier* (Sutton, 2007)

Swinson, Arthur, *North-West Frontier: People and Events, 1839–1947* (Corgi, 1969).

Tanner, Stephen, *Afghanistan: A Military History from Alexander the Great to the Present* (Da Capo Press, 2003).

First Afghan War

Bruce, G., *Retreat from Kabul* (Mayflower, 1967)

Durand, Sir Henry Marion, *The First Afghan War and its Causes* (Lancer Publishers, 2009)

Forbes, Archibald, *Britain in Afghanistan: The 1st Afghan War, 1839–42* (Leonaur, 2007; orig. pub. 1892)

Intelligence Branch Army Headquarters India, *Frontier and Overseas Expeditions from India: Vol. III – Baluchistan and First Afghan War, 1838–1842* (Uckfield, East Sussex, Naval and Military Press, 2006; orig. pub. 1910)

Kaye, J. W., *History of the War in Afghanistan* (Richard Bentley, 3 vols, 1857)

Macrory, Patrick, *Retreat from Kabul: The Catastrophic British Defeat in Afghanistan, 1842* (Lyons Press, 2002).

Norris, James, *First Afghan War, 1838–1842* (Cambridge University Press, 1967)

Second Afghan War

Atwood, Rodney, *The March to Kandahar* (Pen and Sword, 2008)

Balfour, Lady Betty, *The History of Lord Lytton's Indian Administration, 1876–1880* (Longmans, 1899)

Brereton, Captain F. S., *With Roberts to Candahar: A Tale of the Afghan War* (Blackie, 1920)

Cardew, F. G., ed., *The Second Afghan War: Official Account* (Calcutta, Army Headquarters, India, 1908)

Forbes, Archibald, *Britain in Afghanistan: The 2nd Afghan War, 1878–80* (Leonaur Ltd, 2007; orig. pub. 1892)

Hanna, Col. H. B., *The Second Afghan War* (Constable, 1910)

Hensman, Howard, *The Afghan War, 1879–80* (London, 3 vols., W. H. Allen, 1881)

James, D., *Lord Roberts* (Hollis, 1954)

Low, Charles Rathbone, *Major-General Sir Frederick Roberts* (Uckfield, East Sussex, Naval and Military Press, 2002; orig. pub. 1883)

Maxwell, Leigh, *My God – Maiwand! Operations of the South Afghanistan Police Force, 1878–1880* (Leo Cooper, 1979)

Robson, Brian, *The Road to Kabul: The Second Afghan War, 1878–1881* (Spellmount, 2003)

Shadbolt, S. H., *The Afghan Campaigns of 1878–80* (London, 2 vols, 1892)

Stacpoole-Ryding, Richard J., *Maiwand: The Last Stand of the 66th (Berkshire) Regiment in Afghanistan, 1880* (The History Press, 2008)

Third Afghan War

Army Headquarters India, *Third Afghan War 1919: Official Account* (East Sussex, Naval and Military Press, 2004).

Robson, Brian, *Crisis on the Frontier: The Third Afghan War and the Campaign in Waziristan, 1919–20* (Spellmount, 2004).

Memoirs, Journals and First-hand Accounts

Male, Rev. Arthur, *Scenes through the Smoke* (Naval and Military Press, 2003)

Roberts of Kandahar, Earl, *Forty-One Years in India* (Naval and Military Press, 2002; orig. pub. 1905).

Sale, Lady Florentia, *A Journal of the First Afghan War* (Oxford Paperbacks, 2002; orig. pub. 1843)

Index